Snake Hunting!

You creep towards Viper with your every muscle tensed, acutely aware of every molecule on the floor that might betray you with a noise. Your eyes flit from your feet to the door and back again as you tiptoe to where you can see the serpentine villainess.

So much depends on capturing Viper. You think of all the destruction she has caused, the number of times she has tried to kill you . . .

Behind you, a resounding THWACK indicates that Agent Hoffman has caught Blacklash unaware. Viper spins about, sees you, and raises her gun – a dangerous-looking energy weapon.

Will you catch her? Will you survive?

You hurl your shield at her. Make a Shield FEAT by rolling one die and adding the result to your Shield ability. If the total is 18 or less, move on to **33**. If it is 19, 20, or 21, proceed to **197**. If the total is 22 or more, turn to **79**.

Whatever the outcome, only your decisions, and the luck of the dice roll, can help you protect your country from the **Rocket's Red Glare**

MARVEL SUPER HEROES™

CAPTAIN AMERICA®

Gamebook #2

ROCKET'S RED GLARE

by

Kate Novak

Illustrated by Alan Kupperberg
and Pat Redding

PUFFIN BOOKS

To my dearest Jeff,
who leaves his "What Ifs"
just lying around

PUFFIN BOOKS

Penguin Books Ltd, 27 Wrights Lane, London W8 5TZ (Publishing and Editorial)
and Harmondsworth, Middlesex, England (Distribution and Warehouse)
Viking Penguin Inc., 40 West 23rd Street, New York, New York 10010, USA
Penguin Books Australia Ltd, Ringwood, Victoria, Australia
Penguin Books Canada Ltd, 2801 John Street, Markham, Ontario, Canada L3R 1B4
Penguin Books (NZ) Ltd, 182–190 Wairau Road, Auckland 10, New Zealand

First published by Marvel Comics Group, a division of Cadence Industries Corporation 1986
Published in Puffin Books 1987

Printed and bound in Great Britain by
Cox & Wyman Ltd, Reading

FACE FRONT, TRUE BELIEVERS!

In this new role-playing gamebook, you are the shield-wielding Captain America as he encounters one of the most slippery, and deadly, criminals of the Marvel Universe.

Based on the popular MARVEL SUPER HEROES Role-Playing Game from TSR, Inc., MARVEL SUPER HEROES Adventure Gamebooks require only a single standard, six-sided die; a pen or pencil; a moderate supply of luck; and, most of all, your own personal skill in making decisions as you play the game. If dice are not available, you can consult page twelve for a simple alternative requiring only pencil and paper.

MARVEL SUPER HEROES Adventure Gamebooks have been designed to read easily, without complicated rules to slow down the story. Once you finish reading the rules that follow, you should seldom find it necessary to refer back to them. Your choices are clearly stated at each choice point, with occasional reminders of additional options you have available.

Your adventure reads like a book, plays like a game, and offers thrill a minute—with YOU as your favorite MARVEL SUPER HERO!

YOUR CHARACTER

Your real name is Steve Rogers. Born during the Depression, you were a frail youth—too weak to be accepted into the U.S. Army when World War II broke out. But patriotic even then, you volunteered to test a Super-Soldier formula for the government. Though never duplicated since, the experiment was successful in your case, and your body became as physically perfect as a human body can be.

After your transformation, you were given special training in the mental and physical skills required of a twentieth-century warrior. You, Captain America, became America's most effective special operative during the war, defending freedom at every opportunity, until in the final days of the war, you were accidentally frozen in a state of suspended animation.

Awakened decades later by another accident of fate, you found yourself in an America very different from the one you left, but still a nation of free and independent people, and you determined that it was, as ever, your job to keep America that way.

In this adventure, you will discover a diabolical plot that threatens your land's liberty, and it will be up to you, Captain America, to stop it.

PLAYING THE GAME

The MARVEL SUPER HEROES portrayed in this series of books have certain powerful abilities far beyond those of the average human being. As Captain America, your special abilities, which will allow you to attempt feats a normal person wouldn't even consider, are listed on the removable **MARVEL SUPER HEROES Stats Card** located at the front of this book. The Stats Card lists everything you need to keep track of in order to play the game in this book. At the same time, it doubles as a handy bookmark.

SCORING

Playing the game requires that you keep track of three things—**Skill points**, **Karma points**, and **Health points**—on the Super Hero Stats Card located at the front of this book. An explanation of each of these follows.

HEALTH POINTS

Health points represent your general health or life strength. If you are injured or become ill, you lose some of these points. If you lose all of your Healtn points, you will fall unconscious and possibly even die. At any rate, if your Health points drop to zero or less, your adventure is over.

If you are hurt or sick, you may regain some or all of your Health points by spending Karma, which is explained in the following section. Always remember, however, that it is not possible to regain more Health points than you had at the start of the game.

Captain America begins his adventure with a total of 28 Health points.

KARMA POINTS

Karma points represent the effects your actions will have on your future. You earn Karma by doing heroic deeds, by making the right decisions, and in general by being a good person. Conversely, if you do things you shouldn't, you may lose Karma. There is no limit to the number of Karma points you can earn, but you will do better if you spend your Karma rather than hoard it.

You may spend Karma on any die roll you make to increase your chance of success. Here is how it works:

You must make your decision to spend Karma *before* you roll the die.

Once you commit yourself to spending Karma on a die roll, you *must* spend at least 2 Karma points. You may add as many more Karma points as you need to make your die roll successful, providing you have enough Karma points to spend.

If you decide to spend Karma on your die roll but fail the roll because you didn't have enough Karma points to spend or because you choose not to spend that much Karma, you still lose the original 2 Karma points.

Karma may also be spent to regain lost Health points whenever you reach a choice point in the story, unless the text specifically states otherwise. For every Karma point you decide to spend in this manner, increase your total Health score by 1 point. Be sure to subtract the same number from your Karma total. Health points may *not* be converted to Karma points.

Captain America begins this adventure with a total of 12 Karma points.

ABILITY POINTS

Ability points determine how easy or difficult it is for you to perform certain actions, called **FEATS**. Whenever you are asked to attempt a particular type of FEAT, consult the ability called for on your MARVEL SUPER HEROES Stats Card, roll one die, and add the result of the die roll to your Ability score. The text will indicate what you should do next, according to what your total was.

The abilities used in this gamebook are described below.

FIGHTING determines how good you are in armed and unarmed combat. You have had extensive combat training and are, therefore, better able than most people to defend yourself and others.

AGILITY is a measure of your coordination. The Super-Soldier serum has made you more agile than any Olympic athlete. The combination of your talent and training make you better able than most to dodge away from danger, catch things hurled toward you, or leap exceptional distances.

STRENGTH determines how much damage you inflict when you hit something. It also tells how much weight you are able to lift. Although you do not possess superhuman powers, you are exceptionally strong for a human, so you must be careful not to hit people so hard that you cause extensive physical damage or death.

ENDURANCE is a measure of how long you can exert yourself physically without resting or when injured. Consequently, it also determines how well you can stand up to punishment, how long you can hold your breath, and how well you are able to resist the effects of trauma or poison.

REASON reflects how well you can solve problems. You have had a good education and considerable training, so your reasoning skills are above average.

INTUITION gauges how well you observe with your senses and are able to act on that knowledge. Your experiences have made you an acute observer of your surroundings, and your strong moral intuition often alerts you when something is not as it should be.

PSYCHE is based on your willpower and inner strength. A high psyche score will make you resistant to magic and mind control. Your psyche is above average for a human being.

SHIELD is a special skill belonging just to you. You carry a shield made of a unique adamantium and vibranium alloy. If you are behind it, it will absorb tremendous damage and keep you from getting hurt. Because of the practice you have had, you generally throw it with uncanny accuracy and are able to hit opponents with it to knock them off balance or disable them. You are often able to catch your shield on the rebound.

PLAYING WITHOUT DICE

Should you ever wish to play the adventure when dice are unavailable, there is a simple substitute that requires only pencil and paper. Simply write the numbers 1 through 6 on separate slips of paper and mix them up in a container. When a FEAT roll is called for, draw one of the slips, note the number, and place the slip back in the container. Each draw represents one roll of a die.

You, as Captain America, are now ready to face the dangers threatening your country by the ROCKET'S RED GLARE.

Turn to page 13 to begin your adventure. Good luck, and good choices!

As you walk across the plush carpeting in the **1** hallways of the Avengers Mansion, you feel more anxious than ever to hit the streets. The Avengers meeting seemed to drag on today, possibly because you were so eager for it to adjourn, yet as a long-time member of the Avengers, you realize the importance of these meetings. Due in part to its organized nature, including its regular meetings, the band of superheroes known as the Avengers has gained official recognition by the U.S. government and many international agencies, and also enjoys a positive public reputation.

All you can think about today, though, is prowling New York City for possible dangers to the citizens you have sworn to protect. *It's been a slow week for crime,* you reflect. *I shouldn't be disappointed, but I can't shake this feeling that this is only the calm before the storm. I wonder if SHIELD has any information about what's brewing in the underworld?*

In your battles against super foes, you and other Avengers have worked many times with the government organization called SHIELD (Supreme Headquarters International Espionage Law-enforcement Division). SHIELD's director, former U.S. Army colonel Nick Fury, is one of your closest friends. *If I don't turn up anything more interesting by tonight, I'll give Nick a call,* you decide.

Just as you reach the mansion's Fifth Avenue exit, you hear a voice call out behind you, "Cap! Wait just a minute, would you, please?"

As you turn, you see the slim figure of Janet Van Dyne, alias the Wasp, heading toward you through the foyer. The Wasp, as a founding member of the Avengers, is not a woman to be taken lightly. She is also your friend, so you summon up enough patience to listen cordially to what she has to say.

"The team hasn't had a chance to practice much with our star-spangled member recently," she says with a smile as she knocks teasingly on the shield strapped to your back. "I was hoping to interest you in a round of mixed doubles with Namor, Captain Marvel,

13

and me."

You pause uncertainly. Mixed doubles is not as innoc-
uous as it sounds. It's Jan's name for one of the more
challenging and competitive combat simulations
developed for the Avengers to practice teamwork.

You know it's extremely important to exercise with
your team, but you have trouble shaking the feeling
that outside the security of the Avengers Mansion,
something requiring your attention is happening.

If you decide to decline the Wasp's offer and seek the
source of your concern now, turn to **132**. If you want to
accept the Wasp's challenge, turn to **152.**

2 Though you are curious to know what HYDRA is
planning to do with tanks in Philadelphia, the information Agent Bronder has discovered is too valuable to
risk. You must get it to Nick Fury immediately. Hopefully, your escape will also disrupt HYDRA's mission,
whatever it is. "We're going to leave while the odds are
with us," you whisper. "Wait for my signal."

In addition to the other four new HYDRA recruits on
the minibus with you, there is a driver and a guard.
Having watched the other four recruits during training, you feel sure you and the SHIELD agents can take
them out easily, but the guard and the driver are
unknown quantities.

You wait long enough for the van to move several
miles from HYDRA's secret base. Finally, rumbling
noises under the bus's tires, and a series of stops and
starts, indicate to you that the bus must be approaching a toll booth. Slipping your shield out from the back
of your shirt, you signal silently to Bronder and Hoffman to take care of your fellow HYDRA recruits.

Swiftly, you approach the curtain that separates the
front of the bus from the rear. Hoffman and Bronder
each knock out one of the unsuspecting hired thugs.
The remaining two raise an alarm almost immediately.

"What's going on?" one shouts.

"Guard!" the other cries.

14

The moment the guard pokes his head through the curtain, you make a grab for him. To hang on to him, you must make a Strength FEAT by rolling one die and adding the result to your Strength ability. If the total is 8 or less, turn to **139**; if it is 9 or more, move on to **81**.

Your shield strikes Blacklash's arm, startling **3** him. His whip misses the SHIELD agent.

Oblivious to the danger you just saved her from, Agent Bronder flips a switch on her Nitro-buster and holds the nozzle up to the glimmering cloud that is Nitro's gaseous form.

You move toward Blacklash, but Agent Hoffman comes running from the side of the warehouse, tackling the villain before you can reach him. Before Blacklash can recover, Hoffman has him handcuffed, making it impossible for him to wield his weapons.

You stand back, content to watch the two agents at work. "A completely professional job," you congratulate them.

"Did you remember to take Blacklash's teleportation ring off of him?" you ask Hoffman.

In reply, Hoffman just grins and holds up a gleaming wide band set with a large crystal.

"Better leave it over there so Viper doesn't beam you up, Scotty. She eats SHIELD agents," Bronder says.

"I didn't know you cared," Hoffman says, smiling as he complies with his partner's suggestion—not a moment too soon, for the ring glows for a moment and then disappears. Proceed to **147**.

4 *If I stay near Blacklash and the rocket, Nitro won't dare unleash his explosive power for fear of damaging them,* you figure. Although Blacklash has retreated from the battle, cradling his injured arm, you decide he could still be dangerous, so you put the rocket directly between yourself and Nitro.

The elderly villain doesn't act in quite the manner you'd expected, however. He punches a fist at you around the circumference of the missile. You dodge it easily, but Nitro explodes the fist. Your ears ring from the force of the explosion and the rocket wobbles momentarily before settling still again.

"You idiot!" Blacklash yells at his partner. "You'll destroy the rocket!"

Ignoring him, Nitro tries to kick you from around the edge of the rocket. His exploding foot unbalances the rocket again, and it tips toward him.

Lunging backward, you use your shield for cover as the rocket falls to the ground, but the missile remains stable.

"Now it'll never work!" Blacklash screams at Nitro.

The other villain scowls. "I've had enough of this stupid scheme!" he shouts. He blows himself up, not bothering to move farther away from Blacklash. You, fortunately, are farther away from the explosion, but you must subtract 5 Health points from your total.

A dense mist that must be Nitro's gaseous form drifts swiftly across the bay. You turn to question Blacklash, but a peculiar hum fills your ears, and he starts to glow mysteriously. Too late, you realize he has also escaped, using Viper's teleporter.

Turn to **21.**

5 You whip your shield not at Blacklash but at the wall. It ricochets with a cracking sound and slams into the drug-sotted super villain. Blacklash crashes into the table you are strapped to, and you grab hold of his shirt with your bound hand.

A quick blow to the back of his head with your

16

unbound hand and your foe slumps over the top of you. You unfasten the keychain at Scarlotti's belt and open the lock that fastens the metal strap binding your other wrist. Shoving Scarlotti's unconscious form to the ground, you free your legs, as well.

It takes a little while for you to bring Blacklash around, but the look on his face when you do is worth the effort.

"You're going to help me out of here," you explain to him.

"No, way. You're the one who's crazy," he answers groggily.

"Look at it this way, Blacklash. I'm leaving this place, and I'm taking you with me. Now, should I stumble across any guards or, heaven forbid, Viper, they're going to see you're my hostage. They're going to know I defeated you while I was helplessly strapped to a table. They're going to know what a loser you are. Do you want that, Scarlotti? Do you want Viper to see you helpless like that?"

You know from the Avenger's files that Blacklash has a history of manic-depressive psychosis; he is unable to handle his own failure, and his drug-induced state has undoubtedly made him more susceptible to intimidation. Your psychological pounding pays off.

All the fight has gone out of him. Blacklash cringes.

"I'll help you," he whines. "Just don't let her see me, please?"

In almost no time, with your prisoner firmly in hand, you manage to sneak through the maze of Viper's secret base and out into the sunlight.

"This is Pittsburgh, isn't it?" you ask, though you are certain of the riverview and the skyline before you. You've just stepped from a secret passage into the upper station of the Incline, a cable car that climbs the side of Mount Washington. A brass historical plaque confirms your guess. You've battled on this very spot alongside the mighty Avengers.

Across the street you find a phone booth where you place a call to someone you know will be most inter-

17

ested to discover the whereabouts of the Viper—Nick Fury, the director of SHIELD.

"Viper!" Fury sputters. "Did you say you're at Viper's secret base?"

"On top of it actually. With Blacklash. He's been working for her, though right now he's discovering the error of his ways."

"Stay right where you are. I'll have the regional director pick you up. She'll be there in five minutes or she'll be looking for a new job."

The regional director's job seems pretty secure. Within three minutes a helicopter lands in the middle of the street and the pilot waves you in. "Hurry, please, before I get a ticket for an illegal landing and blocking traffic," the woman says.

Within another three minutes the helicopter has landed back on top of the U.S. Steel building, and you are seated in a comfortable office. Blacklash is safely incarcerated.

The helicopter pilot, Sylvia Chansler, turns out also to be the regional SHIELD director. "Colonel Fury's orders were to make you comfortable and to pick your brains at the same time," Director Chansler says.

Quickly, you outline the events of the previous evening, including your capture and subsequent escape.

"Colonel Fury said I was to let you in on everything. To start with, Viper stole these rockets from the government last month and we've been trying to track her ever since. She's been selling them to all sorts of weird groups—terrorists, some of them, but most are hardly what you would describe as extremist. Viper manages to convince them that they need first strike capability against whomever might be their political opposite, or come from a different ethnic group, or just whomever they hold a grudge against. It's quite bizarre."

"How many of these rockets did Viper get?" you inquire.

"Six hundred."

"My lord! She could start a war!" you gasp.

Director Chansler nods. "That's what she's trying to

do, we suspect, but so far we've managed to keep it under wraps. Twenty-two of the rockets have already been used, and should the general public find out, we could have a panic on our hands."

"I don't think you give the public enough credit," you comment.

"Maybe not. SHIELD may reconsider the news black-out if we can just get those rockets back from Viper."

"I see. And what are you doing about it?"

"Basically, I'm waiting for the cavalry."

"The cavalry?"

"We don't keep as large a staff here in Pittsburgh as they do in New York, Captain. We're waiting for Colonel Fury and some of his crack troops to get here. They should arrive within the hour. Care to accompany me to the airport?"

You accept and are standing beside Director Chansler when Nick Fury comes through the gate with two young aides.

"Cap, you never cease to amaze me!" is Fury's first comment. Then he adds, "These are the special officers in charge of recovering the rockets—Ken Hoffman and Laura Bronder. Director Chansler, what's the status?"

"I have mobile units stationed all along the mountainside, sir, just waiting for your people to man them more fully," Chansler replies.

"Fine. There are fifty-four of them waiting on the plane," Fury tells her, "all seasoned agents."

"Great. Agent Lamb will see to them," the woman says, motioning for one of her aides to take charge of the personnel waiting on the army jet. "I'll drive you to Mobile Unit One myself."

Turn to **159.**

6 You launch yourself feet first at the HYDRA agent. Startled by your speed, he has time to aim his rifle at you, but not time enough to get out of your way.

As you connect with his body, his rifle goes off. *He got me,* you realize as your body shudders with pain. Subtract 3 from your Health points.

Can't afford to succumb to the pain, you tell yourself. *I have to stay conscious long enough to protect these people.*

If your Health points have fallen to 0 or less, your adventure ends here. If you have 1 to 5 Health points, you must make an Endurance FEAT by rolling one die and adding the result to your Endurance. If the total is 8 or less, turn to **75**. If it is 9 or more, go to **207**. If you have 6 or more Health points, turn to **153**.

7 The blow you'd intended for the HYDRA commander misses. He didn't get where he is today by being a poor fighter. He dodges your swing and fires his weapon in your direction.

You must subtract 4 from your Health points, as a bullet grazes your side. If your Health is 0 or less, your adventure ends here. If you are still in satisfactory condition, turn to **37**.

8 As you reach your hand into the glowing red basket, a hot, prickly feeling crawls up your skin. You withdraw your hand immediately and remove your glove to discover that your skin is flushed, as though you had just pulled it out of scorching water.

Just then Captain Marvel calls out, "Special Delivery, Cap!" and tosses your shield in your direction. Unfortunately, because of your stinging hand, you flub the catch and your shield spins out of reach.

Beside you, the Sub-Mariner reaches his hand into his team's basket, then pulls it back in a hurry, just as you did. With a snarl, the Atlantean angrily shakes small red flecks of something off his fingers.

Anxiously you turn your attention away from your competition and back to Captain Marvel as she proceeds to try to reach you and the basket. She's done a good job so far of evading the force fields generated by more hovering spheres and taking on other energy forms to pass through metal shields that drop from the ceiling. Now, though, a weapon set in a turret in the ceiling is tracking her with some form of energy beam.

Turn to **195.**

Most of the heat has dissipated from the bombed- **9** out wreckage, of the Staten Island office building. You ask the police officer guarding the site if you may look around.

"Sure, Cap. Gas company turned off the line. Footing could be treacherous, though. Watch yourself."

There is a section of the wreckage where even the ground floor has caved in, revealing some of the basement beneath. Sliding carefully down into the hole, you inspect the only undamaged section of Freedom Flight's ex-headquarters.

The basement is a concrete room, bare but for the wreckage, and smaller than you would have expected considering the size of the building.

Make a Reason FEAT by rolling one die and adding the result to your Reason ability. If the total is 4 or less, move on to **107.** If it is 5 or more, turn to **72.**

"Search for his keys," you order the SHIELD **10** agent as you cross the room swiftly and close the doors silently. Agent Bronder comes up to you a minute later, clasping a heavily laden key chain and a parking card.

Cracking open the door, you check to make sure the corridor is empty. Then, grabbing the keys and Bronder's hand, you dash across the hall to the elevator. The few-second wait for the doors to slide open seems interminably long. Finally, the elevator arrives. You slip a round key into the slot by the parking garage button and turn.

Bronder examines the other keys on the ring. "We're looking for a Cadillac," she says, picking out the ignition and door keys for that model car. "New, too, I'd say, from the lack of wear on the keys."

"Those numbers should correspond to his parking space," you add, pointing to a series of digits along the bottom of the parking card.

You and Bronder meet two surprised HYDRA agents when the elevator doors leading to the underground parking lot open. The two of you make short work of them, though, and as you suspected, the number on the parking tag leads you to the exact slot where the HYDRA agent you met earlier parks his new, white Cadillac.

"Didn't know bad guys could drive white cars," Bronder mutters.

"Hurry and get in. And buckle up," you order, unlocking the passenger door.

You slip in behind the wheel and fasten your seat belt. Trying to avoid suspicion, you drive cautiously up to the mechanical exit gate and insert the parking card. The gate rises and you drive out into the open.

For the first time, you have a look at the entire HYDRA secret base from the outside. It is a large industrial park, isolated from the outside by surrounding farm fields.

"There are armed guards posted at the gate," Bronder gulps, peering at the dimly lit outer gate.

"Yes. We'll have to charge it. Stay down."

You run the Cadillac through the chain-link fence. The guards, apparently accustomed only to keeping people out, are too startled to react immediately. They don't fire until you have passed them. You hear some of the bullets hit the car, and the back windshield cracks into a spiderweb pattern.

"That wasn't too bad," Bronder says, sitting up.

"Down!" you shout, aghast at what lies in the road ahead of you. Across your lane sits an armored tank with a gun mounted on a turret, and the gun is turning in your direction.

Make an Agility FEAT by rolling one die and adding the result to your Agility ability. If the total is 10 or less, go to **193**. If it is 11 or more, turn to **51**.

Blacklash and Nitro must have teleported in to **11** *the warehouse yard*, you think. *That would make sense, since according to the Avengers' file on the Viper, she's been known to give her henchmen special rings so she can track them with her teleporter.*

On each of your vanquished foes, you find just such a ring, each with a large crystal set in a wide band. You remove both of them, and, not sure how they function, you set them on the warehouse loading dock. After a few minutes, the rings glow and then disappear.

"Surprise, Viper," you whisper with a grin. "I'll be coming for you soon, too." Add 5 to your Karma point total.

Within half an hour, SHIELD answers your summons and has an investigation team swarming all over the warehouse yard. The team is headed by no less than the director of SHIELD himself, Nick Fury, a long-time friend and associate.

"Cap," Nick says, shaking your hand, "you never cease to amaze me. How did you do it?"

"I had a tip from Constrictor that something would happen here tonight," you explain, "though he wouldn't say how he knew."

"Excuse me, sir," a young woman in a SHIELD uniform says, tapping Fury on the shoulder.

"What is it, Bronder?"

"Nitro looks pretty sick—apparently some anti-nausea drug Viper gave him is wearing off. Agent Hoffman wants to know if we can send him to the hospital, since he's in no condition to talk."

"What about Blacklash?" Fury asks.

"We can't keep him quiet," she says, grinning. "He's already confirmed a lot of what we suspected."

"What is it you suspected?" you ask Fury.

"Come on." The SHIELD director invites you to follow. "You can listen and learn."

Blacklash sits at a table inside SHIELD's mobile trailer office. He is flanked by two armed security agents, though he is now quite harmless, having been stripped of his armored costume and weaponry.

An agent seated across from Blacklash rises to give Fury his chair.

"Cap," Fury says pointing to the man who just got up, "this is Special Agent Ken Hoffman. Oh, and this is his partner"—Fury indicates the young woman who questioned him earlier—"Laura Bronder. They've been coordinating the hunt for Viper ever since she hijacked a rocket shipment from Uncle Sam last month."

Turn to **201**.

12 The three of you help bring Commander Wright to consciousness to question him. Agent Bronder and Agent Hoffman take a seat on either side of him, and you sit facing him.

Turn to **174**.

Agents Hoffman and Bronder get a SHIELD **13** cleanup crew to take away the rocket, and they tell the authorities as much as they need to know.

After agreeing on a rendezvous point, you, Hoffman, and Bronder part company to get a little rest.

You sleep till mid-morning and awaken feeling refreshed. Add 2 points to your Health. You ride your cycle to the place agreed upon with Agents Bronder and Hoffman the night before, then park next to an unmarked truck trailer that you know is really a SHIELD mobile office. After giving the password, you are ushered inside by Agent Hoffman. Agent Bronder is already sitting inside with SHIELD's director, Nick Fury, an old friend.

"Glad you decided to come in on this with us, Cap," Fury says in greeting.

"If it will stop the Viper, you know you can count on me, Nick."

"Yes," Fury agrees. "Just so you know, we caught Nitro earlier this morning. Viper beamed him into Atlantic City to do some job, but he ran away from her. Didn't like her. He claims he doesn't know a thing about her operation—not even where it's based—because he always got in and out of it via the transporter. I have some other agents working on the only lead he could give us, but I don't think it will pay off as well as Laura and Ken's plan."

"So what is this plan?" you ask.

Turn to **198**.

14 After punching up the appropriate street map on the van's computer-controlled navigation display and locating the Curtis Supply Warehouse, you start up the van's engine. Pleased with the convenience and anonymity of your mobile headquarters, you head toward the Holland Tunnel, listening to a Glenn Miller recording on your tape deck.

Your destination turns out to be a modern facility alongside Newark Bay. The well-lit warehouse yard is surrounded by a high chain-link fence, but from the van you can see no other security defenses.

Using the periscope in the back of the van so you won't be seen, you keep an anxious watch over the warehouse and its surroundings. No one passes you on foot, and motorized traffic on the road is very light.

A few minutes before midnight, you sneak out of the back of the van, intent on having a closer look. Knowing that one of the tools at the Viper's disposal is a matter transmitter, you realize she could transport herself and any of her henchmen inside beyond the locked gate without being detected. She could already be in there. Swiftly, you cross the street and climb over the fence, determined to have a closer look at the warehouse.

Being careful to keep low, you cross the warehouse yard and peer around the side of the building. On the loading dock, you recognize three forms and all of them mean trouble!

First is the super villain Nitro, a man who can deal deadly blows by exploding parts of his body such as his fists and feet, or even explode his entire body, with the same devastating effects as a bomb! Even worse, after disintegrating himself in this manner, he can reform and repeat his attacks over and over, apparently an unlimited number of times. You seem to recall from the Avengers' files that Nitro was supposed to be under guard in a hospital—too ill to use his powers or even stand trial. Obviously someone has freed and cured him. The Viper seems a likely candidate for that role. She has the resources.

The second form is that of Blacklash, whose dangerous cybernetic whips can pierce steel armor or even be made to explode. You have defeated this criminal before, but tonight he is in very tough company.

The third form is what worries you the most. Occupying the attention of the two criminals, towering over them, is an eight-foot-tall, gleaming rocket! Constrictor's nonsense words come back to you, ". . . by the rocket's red glare." He meant it literally. They have a real rocket and it looks as if they are preparing to launch it.

Blacklash is pointing Nitro in the direction of the warehouse. "Go in there," he says, "and wait until I come in to give the all-clear."

"Why do I have to take orders from you?" Nitro growls.

"Because Viper trusted me with her plan and not you," Blacklash snaps.

"Viper, bah!" Nitro spits. "She's just a woman!"

"If it weren't for her, you'd just be an old man lying on your back complaining about the pain. That drug she gave you to help you concentrate enough to explode will wear off soon, so I wouldn't annoy her if I were you, unless you want to end up a prisoner in that hospital again."

Nitro sneers, but he goes into the warehouse as ordered.

So, you think, *Viper has Nitro cowed into submission with some drug that counteracts the nausea that temporarily kept Nitro from exploding. And Blacklash— well, he'd work for anyone. I must try to take out Blacklash without alerting Nitro.*

Sneaking up on Blacklash in the well-lit warehouse yard may be difficult, but you hope he will be too intent on his task of arming the rocket to notice you until it's too late. Perhaps you will do better to surprise him with your shield.

If you want to sneak up on Blacklash and take him on hand-to-hand, move on to **96**. If you'd prefer to throw your shield at him first, turn to **50**.

15 The guard howls with pain as your shield slams into his body, yet he finds the strength to raise his weapon and aim it at you.

"We don't want a lot of noise, now, do we?" you ask, leaping over the bar and grabbing for the weapon.

Make a Strength FEAT by rolling one die and adding the result to your Strength ability. If the total is **7** or less, turn to **86**. If it is 8 or more, turn to **146**.

16 *I have to get that gun away from him*, you think, lunging at your foe. Make a Strength FEAT by rolling one die and adding the result to your Strength. If the total is 7 or less, turn to **68**. If it is 8 or more, go to **137**.

17 "The mobile units are all stationed and at the ready, sir," she informs Fury. "All we needed was the extra units."

"I brought fifty-four seasoned field agents with me. And as an added bonus, Captain America will be helping out. Consider him my second-in-command."

"Pleased to meet you at last, sir. We hear so much about you in training." Director Chansler points out one of her uniformed officers. "Agent Lamb will see that the troops are stationed properly. I'll escort you to Mobile Unit One."

Turn to **159**.

18 In addition to being an important defensive tool, your shield is a pretty handy weapon as well. You spring toward it.

Nearby, the Sub-Mariner has just used some ripped-up floor tiles to create a path through the flames encircling him. With a grin, he gives your shield a kick, but you land on it before it can slide very far away.

With your shield on your arm and the robot behind you, you continue toward your goal.

Turn to **178**.

"I'll take the inside of the warehouse," you **19** decide, hoping it will be the most dangerous place. As brave as Agent Bronder seems, you would not like to see her taking the brunt of the attack from the super villains you are expecting.

"The door is on my side of the building," Bronder explains. "Don't fall asleep," she teases Hoffman before she leads you around to the bay side of the yard.

"Where's your backup?" you whisper.

"Waiting two blocks off for our signal," she answers, patting the walkie-talkie at her waist. "Twenty of them, and some of them are nearly as big as you. I'll be hiding right there," Bronder says as she points into the shadow of the loading dock steps. She leads you up to the loading dock door.

"You're very good at that," you comment, as she picks the door's lock with ease.

"I considered a career in housebreaking, but SHIELD had better health benefits," she replies, holding the door open for you.

"How often do you check in with these?" you ask, holding up the walkie-talkie you were given.

"Every quarter hour, or if we see anything suspicious."

"I don't want you trying to make Nitro blow up on you," you order.

"Don't worry. If I see him first, I'll wait until you arrive and make him blow up on you," she reassures you.

"Good," you reply slipping past her and ducking behind a stack of crates within the building.

Hiding in the quiet, dark warehouse, you feel time is moving unbearably slowly, but before the midnight walkie-talkie check-in is due, Agent Bronder calls in.

"Blacklash, Nitro, and a rocket, just 'beamed' in. Nitro's heading your way, Captain."

There is a bang at the loading dock door. The doorknob falls off and the door swings open, revealing the criminal Nitro.

He must have exploded the lock off by blowing up

29

only his hand, you realize, watching the eerie glow about the villain's fist fade. *We'd better keep this battle outside where there's more room to maneuver.*

Having decided you don't want your opponent entering the warehouse, you charge toward him, hoping to knock him away from the door and off the loading dock. Make an Endurance FEAT by rolling one die and adding the result to your Endurance ability. If the total is 12 or more, go to **82**. If the total is 9, 10, or 11, turn to **36**. If it is 8 or less, move on to **114**.

20 You rush toward your foe with a yell. Make an Endurance FEAT by rolling one die and adding the result to your Endurance ability. If the total is 8 or less, turn to **48**. If it is 9 or more, turn to **166**.

21 *At least I kept them from launching this rocket,* you think. Add 5 to your Karma point total. *Perhaps some experts can tell me something about it.*

You head back to your van and place a call to SHIELD. Within half an hour, an investigation team arrives, headed by no less than the director of SHIELD himself, Nick Fury, a longtime friend and associate.

Fury grins with delight when he spots the rocket. He listens intently to the events of your evening.

"The rocket comes from a whole shipment that Viper hijacked from Uncle Sam last month," Fury explains to you.

"So what was the rocket's target?" you ask. "City Hall, Shield Headquarters, the U.N.?"

"Something much more subtle, but equally dangerous—" Fury begins.

"Excuse me, sir." One of his special agents interrupts him. "We found this man lurking around."

The agent thrusts forth an elderly, rotund man in a three-piece suit.

"Who are you?" Nick Fury snaps.

The man shakes free of the agent holding him and pulls himself up proudly. "I'm Steven Curtis. I own this warehouse."

"What do you know about this rocket?" you ask.

"Nothing," the man replies quickly—too quickly. You're sure he is hiding something.

"Allow me, Cap," Nick Fury says. "You belong to any political organizations, Mr. Curtis?"

The man shifts nervously.

"Come on, I don't have all night," the director of SHIELD barks.

"I'm a founding member of the People's Choice of Latveria," Mr. Curtis mumbles.

Fury sighs. "Let me guess. Viper sold you one of these rockets to fire at some political opponent. Who would that be?"

Mr. Curtis doesn't answer. Instead he hangs his head.

"Your guess, Mr. Hoffman?" Nick Fury addresses the SHIELD agent who brought Mr. Curtis to him.

"The People's Choice of Latveria is a pro-Doom group. Opposing them is Freedom Flight. Their head-quarters is on Staten Island, I believe," Hoffman expounds.

"Just south, across the water," you note.

"I didn't do it," Mr. Curtis gasps. "You've got to believe me. She tried to sell me one of those things, but I refused. 'I'm a man of peace,' I said. She laughed. She said I'd have one whether I wanted it or not, and if I didn't pay her for it, she'd take it out on my warehouse. She's mad! Please, you've got to believe me!"

"Do you see what Viper's trying to do now, Cap?" Fury asks you.

"You mean she's selling these things to political organizations, trying to get them to use them on each other?" you ask.

31

"That's right. And if the organization isn't of a terror-ist bent and refuses her offer, she makes it look like they used it anyway," says Nick.

"Neighborhood weapons escalation." You shiver at the insidiousness of the scheme. "Then, as usual, she plans try to take over in the ensuing violence and chaos," you guess.

"Precisely," the SHIELD director answers. "Are you interested in helping us track her down?"

"You can count on me," you assure him.

Turn to **143**.

22 "All right," you agree. "Let's get going."

With a photocopy of Agent Lamb's map in hand, the three of you are escorted to the factory basement where the entrance you selected to the mines is located.

"Boy, is it dark," Agent Hoffman comments.

"And spooky," his partner adds. "Where are the bats?" she jokes.

"The only thing down here is one very large snake," you reply.

You proceed along the passages swiftly until your path is interrupted by an unmarked vertical mine shaft that goes down a long way. The hole cannot be skirted, and although you could probably leap over it, it is unlikely the SHIELD agents could do so.

"Two-man bridge?" you suggest to Agent Hoffman.

The man nods. "You'd better take the top," he says, helping boost you to his shoulders.

"I always hate this maneuver," Agent Bronder mut-ters. "I can't look," she says as you balance on top of Agent Hoffman and prepare to fall across the gap.

You catch the opposite ledge easily.

"Come on, Laura. We don't want to hang around here all day," Agent Hoffman calls.

The female SHIELD agent bounces lightly across your backs and once safely across grabs onto your wrists to steady you as her partner climbs up your

body. You scramble up the ledge.   Agent Bronder looks
quite pale, and not just from the unnatural Illumination
of the flashlight, as she peers down into the chasm you
just crossed.

"You afraid of heights?" you ask her.

"Of course not," she snaps. "That would be stupid."
She pauses and then adds, "I'm afraid of falling DOWN
from heights."

"Come on, let's keep moving,' you order. Soon you
come to a region where the walls are better shored up.
They begin to look smooth and polished.

"Looks like someone's been through here with a
laser cannon," Agent Hoffman notes.

"Undoubtedly Viper," you say, nodding. "She always
gets hold of pretty advanced technology. Better keep it
down now. These tunnels really carry sound."

You come to a staircase. Make an Intuition FEAT by
rolling one die and adding the result to your Intuition
ability. If the total is 10 or less, turn to **120**. If it is 11 or
more, turn to **58**.

23   You try grabbing Blacklash in a full nelson, but he manages to whip his necro-lash away from Agent Hoffman and around your leg. The jolt of electricity the villain sends through his weapon forces you to release him. Subtract 5 from your Health points.

Blacklash backs away quickly, twisting the crystal on his teleporter ring. He glows and disappears.

"Nuts!" Agent Bronder growls from beneath Blacklash's gravity bolo.

"I'm sorry," you apologize.

"It's not your fault," Agent Hoffman says. "We wouldn't have stood a chance without you. At least we still have our contingency plan."

"Yuk," his partner comments as you help disentangle her from the bolo.

"What's the contingency plan?" you ask.

"Well, it requires some undercover work to follow up another tip we have," Hoffman replies, eyeing you thoughtfully.

"Is there anything I can do?" you ask.

"As a matter of fact, we have a way we can fit you in, if you're willing."

"If it means catching Viper, I'm willing," you answer. Turn to **117**.

24   You decide to hit this monstrosity with all you've got, rather than risk having it survive a lighter blow, so you aim your shield at its neck and heave it with all your might.

To attempt this FEAT, roll one die and add the result to your Shield ability. If the total is 19 or less, turn to **93**. If it's 20 or more, turn to **169**.

25   The HYDRA commander is at least as strong as you. He escapes from your hold, and tries to back away so he can use his rifle, but Agent Bronder, having already knocked out her own opponent, jams the butt of her rifle into the commander's knees. He crashes to the floor. You knock him out with a blow to the back of the neck. Add 1 to your Karma points for helping to defeat and capture the HYDRA commander.

Rifle fire echoes through the warehouse, and bullets ricochet off the back of your 'turtle shell.' Turn to **69**.

Having lost Blacklash, you spin about quickly **26** to check on the unconscious Nitro.

"I took off his teleportation ring," Laura Bronder explains. "I put it on the ground, and it disappeared. Just think, if I'd held onto it, I could be giving Viper your regards right now."

"You may not have lived long enough. Viper is smart enough to have an ambush waiting," you warn. "Anyway, I'd prefer to greet her in person, thank you. It's a shame we lost Blacklash. He would have known more about Viper's operation."

"Yes," Hoffman agrees. "Still, Nitro might know something useful."

"I just gave him a shot to be sure he stays unconscious until the backup gets here with the energy-absorbing cuffs," Bronder tells you.

"Fine," you answer.

"Oh," Hoffman adds, "I caught someone by the name of Steven Curtis skulking around out back. Says he's the owner of the warehouse. Claims Viper's trying to frame him."

"He might have been here to buy the rocket," Bronder guesses.

"I don't think so. He hasn't got any money on him," Hoffman replies.

"Maybe Nitro will know something about him," you suggest.

"Tell me—why does that rocket have a U.S. Government stamp on it?" You point to the missile brought in by Viper's henchmen.

"Oh, did we forget to mention that?" Hoffman asks, shrugging. "Viper hijacked these rockets from Uncle Sam. Got away with over six hundred of them."

35

"Six hundred!" you gasp.

"And if Blacklash figures out how to copy the electronic components, Viper could be making more within the year," Hoffman points out.

You shake your head in shock. "Better move your backups forward. We've got to get some answers out of Nitro—fast!" you order.

"Yes, sir."

Nitro is not particularly excited about cooperating with SHIELD, but apparently he has little liking for Viper, either. Unfortunately, there isn't much he can tell you. He himself was virtually a prisoner in Viper's hideout because she wasn't about to trust him until he proved himself. He was always transported in and out of her hideout with Blacklash by way of Viper's matter transmitter, so he can't even tell you where the hideout is.

"We have got to get a fix on that woman. There must be something you can tell us, Nitro," you insist.

"She only goes out to collect money for the rockets," the elderly villain shrugs. "Catch her making a sale."

"Unfortunately, she doesn't send us engraved invitations to these events," Hoffman mutters.

"She'll be selling a rocket day after tomorrow to Freedom Flight," Nitro volunteers.

"What's Freedom Flight?" you ask.

"Some dumb group we were supposed to hit with this rocket tonight. Their headquarters is on Staten Island. We were supposed to make it look like the guy who owns this place did it, 'cause Viper couldn't convince him to buy a rocket. I was supposed to blow up his warehouse to teach him a lesson."

"What made Viper think Mr. Curtis would want to hit Freedom Flight with a rocket?" you ask.

"Beats me," Nitro shrugs.

"I can answer that," Hoffman says. "Curtis belongs to some group called the People's Choice of Latveria. They're all gung-ho on Victor Von Doom. Freedom Flight is trying to get him deposed."

"Why would anyone support Victor Von Doom?" you

ask. "He's a power-mad would-be world conqueror."

"Yep," Agent Bronder nods. "But he's done pretty good things to the Latverian economy, and the Latverians have, unfortunately, had worse leaders than Doom."

"I see."

"It doesn't matter anyway," Bronder continues. "Once Viper's learned that we've captured Nitro, she'll change her plans on this sale."

"No," Nitro insists. "She doesn't know that I know. I eavesdropped on her and Blacklash. They were going to meet someone in some secret passage at Freedom Flight's Staten Island headquarters."

"But you were going to bomb it," Bronder argues.

"I only know what I heard," Nitro says, shrugging. "She told Blacklash the Staten Island headquarters."

"It's worth a try," you urge the SHIELD agents.

"I guess so," Hoffman admits.

Add 3 points to your Karma for helping to capture Nitro and the rocket, then turn to **98**.

With a thrust of your feet on the floor and your **27** arms gripping her wrists, you toss Viper over your head. Both of you rise to your feet simultaneously and circle each other warily.

Viper makes a move for a dart at her weapon's belt just as you whisk your shield up from the floor. Viper keeps her darts coated with the same deadly poison she secretes from her fangs. She throws one of the projectiles, but you block the miniature missile with your shield.

Turn to **115**.

28 Inspecting your fallen foe's pouch, you find his gravity bola, a weapon that generates an artificial gravity field that will weight anyone entangled in it to the ground. You wrap it carefully around its owner. Add 5 points to your Karma total for defeating Blacklash.

Now, how patient can Nitro be? you muse, flattening yourself against the wall by the door to the warehouse.

Not very, you think in answer to your own question, when, less than three minutes later, you hear Nitro approaching the door, muttering to himself.

"What's keeping you, Blacklash?" the explosive man hisses from the door.

You hold your breath, poised for action. The moment Nitro sticks his head out the door, you clobber him with your shield and he collapses beneath you.

I don't like ambushing my foes, you think as you check Nitro's vital signs, *but I haven't much choice if they insist on playing with rockets.* You tie Nitro up with Blacklash's whips. *That won't hold him if he wakes up and explodes,* you tell yourself, *but maybe the drug Blacklash mentioned will have worn off by then and Nitro won't be able to use his power again.*

Make a Reason FEAT by rolling one die and adding the result to your Reason ability. If the total is 4 or less, turn to **109**. If it is 5 or more, go on to **11**.

29 "Get me something to tie this man up—" you start to say, when in a sudden burst of power, the HYDRA leader breaks your hold. He turns the rifle back on you just as the double agent Hoffman tackles him.

Your foe fires at you as he falls to the floor. You feel a bullet graze your forehead.

You must subtract 1 point from your Health, and go to **207**.

30 You hit the guard feet-first. As you pull yourself up into a guarded stance, your opponent remains lying on the floor. Turn to **184**.

You and your partner reach the other side of the **31** room after evading several less deadly obstacles such as nets, walls, and rubber bullets. Your team's goal turns out to be a cannonball weighing more than two hundred pounds. Grinning, Captain Marvel watches you lift it out of the basket. "Promise not to drop it on my toes," she says, "and I'll run interference for you."

The two of you can claim the bonus for being the first to get your ball back to the finish line, but, in the end, the Wasp and Namor score the most total points.

"I'm afraid it's my fault, C.M.," you apologize, looking with chagrin at the head of your robot opponent. "I was too rough."

Wasp picks up the metal head. "Alas, Robbie Robot, I knew him, Namor. He won us the game."

"We'll give you a chance to prove yourself again," Namor offers. "Next week, if you can make it."

"Seems as if I should give it a try," you agree. "Until then. Good afternoon, Avengers."

Turn to **172.**

Agent Hoffman hails a state police car parked **32** next to the toll booth. You are waiting by the bus with Agent Bronder, holding onto your prisoner, when you feel three rapid bangs on your shield.

"Gunfire!" you shout. "Stay down!" Shoving your prisoner and Agent Bronder out of the way, you spot the sniper—the HYDRA bus driver.

As you leap back toward the bus, your attacker fires all the ammunition left in his weapon at you, but the bullets bounce off your shield. As he tries frantically to reload, you stun him with a punch and confiscate the gun.

You identify yourself to the New Jersey State Troopers by revealing your Captain America costume under the phony super villain suit, and Agents Hoffman and Bronder recite a special code that identifies them as SHIELD agents. At your request the police take all of the HYDRA agents into custody. Give yourself 1 Karma

Point for helping to capture them and for keeping them from participating in the assault in Philadelphia.

Half an hour later, Nick Fury lands a SHIELD air car at the state trooper barracks where you've been waiting for him. "I take it by your smiling faces that you have good news for me," the SHIELD director says.

"Viper's base is in Pittsburgh," Bronder answers.

"Good work," Fury comments. "You can give me the details on the way there. Excuse me for a minute while I speak with the local police and make sure that you three are free to leave."

After speaking with the police and the prisoners for another half an hour, the SHIELD director joins you again. "They're letting you go for good behavior, but remember, I can send you back any time," Fury jokes.

As you leave the police station and walk toward Fury's air car, the director says, "The HYDRA guard you captured said that the raid you were supposed to be on was to capture Viper at Freedom Flight's political headquarters in Philadelphia."

"With tank crews?" you ask. "Isn't that a little heavy handed, even for HYDRA?"

Fury nods. "Especially considering Viper wasn't even there. Just before I left New York, I had a report that she was trying to sell a rocket to a Freedom Flight member in a secret cellar beneath Freedom Flight's former headquarters on Staten Island. There was some sort of fight over money. Viper escaped, but Blacklash was shot by the would-be customer. He's in intensive care, so he isn't talking just yet."

"But if Viper doesn't know that, she could be planning to change her base right now," you figure.

"That's right," Fury agrees. "All the more reason to get going right now."

Turn to **40**.

33 Viper fires her gun just as your shield comes spinning toward her. Though the weapon's energy blast cannot harm the disk, it is sufficiently powerful to deflect it. Your shield crashes to the ground and the energy beam charges toward you.

You feel as though your chest is on fire. Subtract 6 points from your Health. You see the beam disintegrating as the weapon's power pack wears down, but it's hard to convince your body that the force is gone. It's hard just to breathe.

If you have 10 or fewer Health points, you must make an Endurance FEAT by rolling one die and adding the result to your Endurance ability. If the total is 8 or less, turn to **160**. If the total is 9 or more, or if you still have more than 10 Health points, turn to **55**.

Your tactic isn't totally successful. You duck **34** quickly, and Nitro's exploding fist knocks his partner back, but you are not fast enough to avoid the brunt of his attack. Your head is ringing from the shock wave, and a searing heat travels across your neck. Subtract 6 from your Health point total.

Furthermore, you now find yourself entangled in Blacklash's gravity bola, and you are being dragged to the ground.

Make an Endurance FEAT by rolling one die and adding the result to your Endurance. If the total is 10 or less, turn to **90**. If it is 11 or more, move on to **122**.

After binding your ankle, you rise and begin **35** carving footholds in the slick wall with your shield. In light of your injury, climbing and balancing is so difficult that you do not succeed in the first three attempts. You sit in the mine shaft for a moment taking deep breaths. The cool air seems to invigorate you. Summoning your strength for a fourth time, you finally manage to scramble to the top.

After a brief rest, you test your ankle. It's painful, but not useless. You limp determinedly down the tunnel, leaving Viper's phantom staircase behind.

Turn to **100**.

36 You slam into Nitro, knocking him away from the door. Surprised, the exploding super villain does not react immediately, and so you get another chance to hit him.

Turn to **45**.

Yanking your shield out from the pocket on the **37**
back of your shirt, you charge toward the HYDRA commander. His rifle shot rattles harmlessly against your
shield, and his eyes widen as it finally dawns on him
who you really are.

Make an Endurance FEAT by rolling one die and adding the result to your Endurance ability to knock down
your foe. If the total is 9 or less, turn to **212**. If it is 10 or
better, turn to **43**.

Your shield bounces off the robot's ankle with **38**
no apparent effect. Fortunately, just as the mechanoid's blades slash down at you, you catch your shield
on the rebound. As you raise it over your head to block
the robot's deadly blow, you realize that now you must
dodge or risk being hit by one of the robot's other fiend-
ish appendages. Turn to **64**.

By noon, the military jet commandeered by **39**
Nick Fury has landed at Pittsburgh's Allegheny
County Airport. You are greeted at the gate by
SHIELD's regional director for the area, Sylvia
Chansler.

"I'm glad to be able to give you some good news,
Colonel Fury," she begins. "We caught Blacklash—
Mark Scarlotti—less than ten minutes ago."

"Congratulations. How did you manage that?" Fury
asks.

"Luck mostly. We posted a lookout within minutes
after your phone call, and we spotted Scarlotti coming
out of the Incline's lower station, in civilian dress. Without his costume, he couldn't give us too much trouble.
He was heading for the Pirates game at Three Rivers
Stadium."

"Very good," says Fury. "If Viper gave him the day
off, it's likely she isn't expecting us."

"Unless she's planning on leaving him behind," you
suggest.

"You might be right," the head of SHIELD agrees. "Are you prepared, Chansler?" he asks his regional director.

Turn to **17**.

40 You hop into Nick Fury's SHIELD aircar with Agents Bronder and Hoffman and he lifts off from the street toward Philadelphia International Airport.

"Oh, Cap," Fury adds, "thought you'd like to know just one other little piece in this puzzle that we've managed to fit in."

"What's that, Nick?" you ask.

"Constrictor's part. We found out from one of the other captured HYDRA agents that Constrictor was the one who told HYDRA that Viper had stolen the rockets they had coveted for themselves."

"How did Constrictor know?"

"It seems sometime last week Constrictor was at the Curtis Supply Warehouse, and he overheard Viper and Blacklash trying to intimidate someone into buying one of these rockets."

"What was Constrictor doing there?"

"Stealing something on consignment for HYDRA," Fury answers.

"Which explains why he was so elusive about what he knew," you say. "Well, at least he had the good sense to involve me in it and not just leave it up to HYDRA."

"I'll second that," Agent Hoffman comments.

"I'll third it," Agent Bronder adds.

Turn to **186**.

You know you need to put this robot out of **41**
action, but you'd like to keep from losing points by
destroying it. Without further hesitation, you fling
your adamantium shield at the robot's left ankle.

To attempt this FEAT, roll one die and add the result
to your Shield ability. If the total is 19 or less, turn to
38. If it's 20 or 21, turn to **125**. If it's 22 or more, turn to
80.

You decline the sergeant's advice about seeing **42**
a doctor. You don't think anything is broken. You just
feel a little stiff and sore from being smashed about.

Donning a fresh uniform, you walk back to investigate the ruins of Freedom Flight's former headquarters. Turn to **9**.

You crash into the HYDRA agent, and he slams **43**
into the wall, his rifle clattering on the floor. Agent Hoffman retrieves it. Add 2 to your Karma points for
defeating this high-level HYDRA operative.

You check on the other HYDRA guard in the room,
who met more than his match in Agent Hoffman. *He'll
be out for a while*, you note. Turn to **92**.

Your target is standing too close to the rocket, **44**
causing your shield to bounce off the missile's curved
surface without hitting Blacklash. Startled, the villain

looks up with a shout.

You just have time to scoop up your shield as Black-lash pulls out his whip. It lashes across the adaman-tium disk with a loud crack.

Turn to **73**.

45 Nitro backs away from you, his eyes starting to glow—an indication he is about to explode! Even though this will give Agent Bronder a chance to use her Nitro-buster, you would prefer to take the villain out before he can cause any damage.

You aim a kick at his midsection. Make this Fighting FEAT by rolling one die and adding the result to your Fighting ability. If the total is 13 or less, turn to **59**, if it is 14 or more, go to **183**.

46 You don't quite clear the expanse of the chasm, but you manage to grab hold of the opposite ledge—just barely! After hauling yourself up to the top you take a short breather before continuing. Soon, you come to a region where the walls are better shored up. They begin to look smooth and polished, as though they were cut out by some special technology not yet in general use.

"This must be some of Viper's excavations," you decide.

Then you come to a staircase leading up. Make an Intuition FEAT by rolling one die and adding the result to your Intuition ability. If the total is 10 or less, turn to **131**. If it 11 or more, go to **196**.

Now that you are committed to the game, you **47** feel good about agreeing to play. You learn something from every team practice session and teach others at the same time. Add 1 Karma point to your total.

A melodic tone sounds, signaling the start of the contest. Wasp immediately shrinks to a near-invisible half-an-inch high as Namor rushes forward heedlessly. You are pleased to see that Captain Marvel shows more caution and inspects the walls first. Still, one can't be too cautious.

"Time to get our feet wet, C.M.?" you say.

"Is that what the Sub-Mariner is doing?" your partner says with a giggle as several nozzles, shooting jets of flame, spring from hidden panels in the floor, blocking Namor's path. Gasping in surprise, the Atlantean backpedals to avoid the fiery fountain.

Your amusement is cut short, however, as you spot a basketball-sized sphere drifting down from the ceiling. You recognize the sinister, high-pitched whine emanating from the sphere as a force-field barrier—something that could trap both you and your partner.

"Heads up, lady!" you shout, pointing at the object hovering toward your partner. "Standing still isn't safe either!" you warn her as you leap aside to avoid capture by the force field.

Out of the corner of your eye, you spot several tiny, weighted squares of mosquito netting dropping from the ceiling. You hear the Wasp growl as she resumes her full size in order to throw off one of the insect-size traps.

A waist-high wall pops up from the floor. Just as you are vaulting over it, you notice that something very tall has emerged from a door in the side wall and that the very tall something is quickly closing in on you. Taking a defensive crouch, you hurriedly study this potential foe. It's a seven-foot, metal-plated robot, bristling with gleaming, razor-sharp appendages!

Attempt an Intuition FEAT by rolling one die and adding the result to your Intuition ability. If the total is 10 or less, turn to **182**. If it's 11 or more, turn to **70**.

48 Commander Wright dodges your charge at the last moment, and you go flying off the edge of the tank. Overhead you hear the sound of rifle fire, and a second later the HYDRA leader comes crashing down from the tank, shot dead.

For a sickening moment, you think Agent Hoffman might have killed him instead of trying to capture him alive, but you spot Hoffman, still on the floor of the warehouse, locked in hand-to-hand combat with the other veteran HYDRA agent. Emerging from the hatchway of the opposite tank is a new HYDRA operative. He had probably been aiming at you before you took a dive. Instead he hit his own leader—ruining your chance to learn if Commander Wright knew the location of Viper's secret base.

Turn to **61**.

49 As you leave the building with Agents Hoffman and Bronder, a SHIELD aircar drops down in front of you. The director of SHIELD, Nick Fury himself, alights, greeting you with high spirits. "We just captured Blacklash," he tells you. "He was helping Viper sell a rocket to Freedom Flight in Staten Island, and got himself shot."

"By Aaron Gress?" you ask.

"Yes, Mr. Gress got angry when Viper wouldn't show him a rocket without him showing her the cash first," Fury confirms. "Blacklash is in intensive care and won't be talking for days. What do you have for me?" he asks his agents.

"Viper's secret base is in Pittsburgh," Agent Bronder answers proudly.

"Well, then, let's get to the airport before she breaks camp," says Fury. "You coming, Cap?"

"I wouldn't miss it," you declare.

Turn to **40**.

Quickly slipping from behind the corner of the **50** building, you take careful aim at Blacklash and heave your star-emblazoned shield in his direction.

Make a Shield FEAT by rolling one die and adding the result to your Shield ability. If the total is 21 or more, turn to **155**. If the total is 19 or 20, go to **135**. If it is less than 18, turn to **44**.

You swerve your car into the opposite lane just **51** as a bright light flashes from the tank. You hear a shell explode behind you as you speed past the armored vehicle. Once beyond it, you know it will never be able to catch you.

"Do you think he was just trying to signal you to turn off your brights?" Agent Bronder jokes.

"I think he was trying to turn off my brights permanently," you answer.

Turn to **133**.

"First, I thought you'd be interested to know," **52** Nick Fury begins as soon as you are seated in his office an hour later, "that Nitro quit Viper yesterday. She sent him to Atlantic City for some mission, and he got tired

49

of taking orders. Chucked his teleporter ring. Then we caught him. The only thing is, he can't tell us much. He says he never knew where he was, since Viper would only let him in and out via the teleporter.

"At least we have one less super-powered hireling to worry about where Viper's concerned," you note.

"True," Fury replies. "Unfortunately, the big worry is enough. There were six hundred rockets on the shipment Viper hijacked from Uncle Sam. And she wasn't the only one after them. HYDRA was trying to get hold of them, as well, but she stole them out from under their nose."

"It's hard to say which would be worse," you reply, thinking of the damage the world crime syndicate HYDRA could do with the rockets, since their ultimate goal is also to rule the world.

"Yes. But HYDRA would have sold most of them overseas, and we know most of HYDRA's customers. Viper's quite mad. You never know what she'll do next," Fury answers. "She's been convincing all sorts of people to buy these rockets— people you wouldn't think of as fanatical or violent, until of course they use their purchases. Viper seems to be trying to start a civil war, and with those rockets, we could have as big a mess over here in America as they have in places like Beirut or Ireland or Central America."

"Yes, I see. She's hoping to topple the government in the resulting chaos, and maybe even seize control. So what's your lead?" you ask.

"We know HYDRA's been trying to get the rockets back from her. They attacked Freedom Flight's headquarters in Philadelphia this morning thinking she would put in an appearance there, but HYDRA's really slipping these days. Viper was at Freedom Flight's old headquarters on Staten Island, making a deal in a secret basement stronghold. The deal went sour, though, and Blacklash got shot. He's in intensive care and won't be talking for a few days."

"And you're afraid Viper will escape before then."

"Or HYDRA will attack her base. They've put it off

50

only long enough to recruit a minor army. So I got two of my agents recruited yesterday. They were supposed to learn Viper's base. HYDRA sent one of them on this Freedom Flight assault this morning. The commander of the mission went bananas when Viper didn't show up. He threatened to shoot everyone in sight, so my man had to blow his cover to stop him."

"That explains why no one was answering the phone at Freedom Flight," you note.

There is a knock on the door and at Fury's command a young man in a SHIELD uniform comes in. The man looks a little battered and very worried.

"Cap, this is Ken Hoffman. The agent I just mentioned. His partner is still undercover at HYDRA, working as a computer technician, and we need you to get her out," says Fury.

Turn to **108**.

You land easily on the roof of the other tank and **53** give the HYDRA commander a quick push. He joins Laura and his fellow HYDRA agent on the floor of the warehouse. You leap down after him, trying to grab him from behind. Make a Strength FEAT by rolling one die and adding the result to your Strength. If the total is 8 or less, go to **32**. If it is 9 or more, proceed to **71**.

When you awaken, you find yourself lying in **54** an ambulance. A woman in a SHIELD uniform is administering an intravenous drip into your arm.

"What happened?" you moan.

"Cap? It's me, Nick," a voice says.

You have a hard time separating the images of two faces, that of the strange woman and a more familiar man's face—the face that goes with the voice.

The woman moves away from you, and slowly your eyes manage to focus on Nick Fury, the director of SHIELD and a longtime friend and associate.

"We found you near a blown-up warehouse."

"Viper," you manage to whisper.

"Viper was there?" Fury asks.

"No," you shake your head. "Her henchmen—Blacklash and Nitro. They had a rocket. It's getting harder to talk," you whisper.

"The nurse gave you something for the pain, Cap," Fury tells you. "You rest now. Don't worry. We'll get Viper and her flunkies."

As you drift back into unconsciousness, you wonder whether Fury and SHIELD will really manage to defeat Viper and her plot, whatever it is.

Your adventure ends here. You know now who your enemy is, and you may begin again, subtracting 1 from your initial Health total and 1 from your initial Karma.

55 "I can't let Viper win this. Bronder and Hoffman have their hands full with Blacklash. If Viper gets past me, we're all dead."

You find the strength, just barely, to lunge for your female foe. Startled, Viper falls back and activates her teleporter ring.

"I WILL destroy you, Captain," she hisses as the glow begins to surround her. "It's only a matter of—" and she disappears.

Turn to **127**.

56 An idea occurs to you, and you ask Agent Bronder, "Have you checked under Madame HYDRA?"

"Well, no. But Viper hasn't gone under that name for ages."

"No, but an organization with the arrogance of HYDRA may not want to admit in their own data banks that she's renounced her allegiance to them."

"You have a point there," Bronder admits. "I'm going to turn in. Say good night to Ken for me."

After eating, you and Agent Hoffman also leave the festivities behind and head back for your dorm rooms.

The next morning, after an early meal somewhat

more austere than last night's dinner, training continues.

After less than an hour, six men, including you and Agent Hoffman, are separated from the main group. You, fortunately, are allowed to remain in your "Turtle" costume, in deference, no doubt, to your skill, but the others are given HYDRA uniforms to dress in—complete with masks.

Then you are taken to the windowless minibus in the underground garage, where Agent Bronder is already waiting. Also dressed in a HYDRA uniform, she is carrying her mask. As soon as she is sure you have seen her, she puts the mask on. All seven of you are loaded onto the minibus. You, Hoffman, and Bronder squeeze into the back seat together.

Amidst the hubbub of speculation among the other newly hired HYDRA agents, Bronder manages to whisper some information. "Madam HYDRA's secret base is in Pittsburgh, Pennsylvania, under something called the Incline."

"Good work," Hoffman whispers back.

"Hey, I owe it to the Turtle here," Bronder admits. "You were right about where I'd find Viper listed—under Madame HYDRA."

"So where are we going?" you ask.

"According to the computer—some assault in Philadelphia, but that's all it would tell me. I had the computer pick my name for a tank crew."

"That's what I call a computer error," Hoffman mutters. "What do you know about tanks."

"What's to know?" Bronder asks. "You put the pedal to the metal, and the tank goes forward over anything in the way."

"Oh, brother."

"I thought it would be easier for us to get away from this little group than from the training base," Bronder whispers, indignant. "We might even want to figure out what HYDRA's up to in Philadelphia."

"Good thinking," you say.

"If I get a vote in this," Agent Hoffman interjects, "I'd

like to leave before HYDRA gives her a tank to play with."

If you want to make your escape as soon as possible, since you already know the location of Viper's secret base, turn to **2**. If you'd rather stick around to find out what HYDRA is up to, turn to **176**.

57 Your shield hits the robot just as you had planned, knocking the mechanical creature to the floor, where its deadly arms continue to thrash about. You feel safe from the creature now, since it appears unable to right itself and follow you. Add 1 Karma point to your total for not damaging the robot.

You are not so lucky with your shield, however. It has rebounded away from you at an awkward angle, allowing Wasp to catch it in midair and toss it out of your immediate reach.

If you think you'd better retrieve the adamantium disk in case you need it again, turn to **18**. If you'd rather race ahead without your shield before the computer sends something else after you, turn to **145**.

58 You pause on the bottom step. The SHIELD agents behind you wait patiently.

"If we climb much higher, we'll be above ground."

"What's the map say?" Bronder asks.

"We went off the edge of that several minutes ago," you inform her. "We're in Viper territory now. Turn off your flashlights for a moment." In the dark, you can see that all the steps from the center of the stairway up glow in the dark. Climbing the lower steps, you turn your light back on to investigate more closely. You touch the first glowing step with your shield. The shield goes right through.

"It's a holographic projection." Lying down, you plunge your head through the light image and investigate what lies beneath. It's a smooth, round pit about fifteen feet deep.

Agent Bronder's head appears next to yours. "There aren't any snakes. I thought pits were supposed to have snakes."

"It doesn't always have to be snakes, Laura," her partner says, sighing.

"It is in the movies."

"Let's keep going, Indiana Bronder," you chuckle. Turn to **154**.

59

Nitro is far swifter than his age would warrant, and he retreats agilely from your attack. Before he can explode, you dodge behind your shield.

The shock wave from Nitro's attack—his whole body discorporealating in a huge release of energy—throws you across the loading dock. Your unwilling flight is stopped the hard way by the side of a truck trailer. Subtract 10 points from your Health. If your Health is 0 or less, your adventure ends here.

If you are still functioning, make an Endurance FEAT by rolling one die and adding the result to your Endurance ability. If the total is 9 or less, go to **65**. If the total is 10 or more, move on to **121**.

60

Your luck fails you as you creep closer to Blacklash. You step on a broken piece of glass, and your quarry looks up, startled by the crunching sound. Blacklash freezes for just a moment as he recognizes you. Then he regains the presense of mind to reach for his whip and shout for his partner. Turn to **73**.

61

SHIELD takes care of mopping up the warehouse after Agent Hoffman calls them on the minibus radio.

Nick Fury informs you that HYDRA was wrong about Viper being in Philadelphia that morning. "She was on Staten Island with Blacklash trying to sell a rocket, but the Freedom Flight member she was trying to sell it to got into an argument with her and shot Blacklash. He's in intensive care. Hopefully we'll be able to get something out of him soon."

Unfortunately, it is a week before Blacklash is able to talk to SHIELD. By the time he gives you the location of Viper's secret base, the villainess has fled. You take some consolation, however, in the fact that there are no more domestic incidents reported involving rockets.

Later in the month, Agents Hoffman and Bronder inform you that apparently HYDRA got the rockets from Viper, after all, and the crime syndicate has been selling the missiles overseas. SHIELD has been able to recover a few because HYDRA is generally easier to track than Viper. Of Viper's whereabouts, they haven't a clue.

"Just once I'd like to capture her," you sigh.

"You still might get a chance someday," Agent Hoffman answers.

"And we'd like to be there when you do," Agent Bronder adds.

Your adventure ends here. You may begin again, subtracting two from your initial Karma total for losing Viper and the rockets.

62 While you are waiting for Freedom Flight's office to open, you dress as Steve Rogers and have breakfast in a local diner. Reading the morning paper as you eat your breakfast, you notice an article buried in the back of the paper that reports that Nitro has been captured by the authorities in Atlantic City.

That should cramp Viper's style a little, you think. *I wonder if Nitro's volunteering any information?*

Later, again in your Captain America costume, you

climb the steps to the run-down townhouse that houses the organization known as Freedom Flight. You are aware of all the faces at windows along the street, watching you. You don't have to knock on the door, it is opened the moment you reach the top step.

A middle-aged man, as harmless-looking as Mr. Curtis, stands before you with his hand out.

"Captain America," the man greets you as you shake his hand. "This is a great honor. I'm Kurt Gress. Welcome to Freedom Flight's new headquarters."

Mr. Gress ushers you into the building's front room. A map and some travel posters of Latveria hang on the walls. Cardboard boxes full of files are stacked along the floor. An old desk, a table, and some folding chairs are the only furniture. There is one telephone.

"Are you the only staff member here, Mr. Gress?"

"The rest are upstairs sleeping. We worked so hard at cleaning the place up and moving into it yesterday that we didn't hear the news about our old headquarters until the evening. Then everyone stayed up arguing."

"Arguing?"

"Well, discussing it. It was really quite shocking. We never thought they would go that far."

"Who?"

"The Latverian Secret Police, of course."

"The rocket was launched from a warehouse belonging to Steven Curtis."

"Naturally. He's one of their tools—him and his People's Choice." Mr. Gress spits the words out with disdain.

"Mr. Curtis claims he isn't responsible. He doesn't impress me as a man of violence."

"He didn't impress me that way either," Mr. Gress admits. "But Aaron had him pegged, I guess. Aaron said Curtis would try something underhanded. Uh—Aaron, that's my cousin. He's the reason I helped start this group. See, my father came here from Latveria. I'm second-generation American, but my father's brother stayed in Latveria. His son, my cousin Aaron, just escaped from there last year."

"I see. Is your cousin here now?"

"Well, no. He had some business to finish up in New York. He'll be here by tonight."

"Mr. Gress, Mr. Curtis claims he was framed because he refused to purchase certain weapons from a terrorist known as the Viper. It's reasonable to assume the Viper might offer you a similar deal so you can strike back in retaliation."

"That's nonsense. We are not a terrorist organization, Captain America. We do not espouse violence. Currently we are only trying to get the U.S. Government to put pressure on the Latverians to free political prisoners and grant due process of law to its citizens. Is that so unreasonable?"

"No, Mr. Gress. But the question is: did your organization's argument last night involve changing your means of attaining those goals in view of the destruction of your original headquarters?"

"Even if it did, I can assure you that as long as I am the head of this organization we will not be resorting to the enemy's tactics."

"A very noble speech, Kurt," a woman with a thick accent says from the hall doorway, "but maybe you'd better take a look out the window."

"We're doomed!" another voice cries.

About six other members of Freedom Flight come running down the hall stairs and line up behind the woman in the doorway. They all look anxiously toward their leader, Kurt Gress.

You run to the window with Mr. Gress. Outside, a modern armored tank is rumbling directly toward you!

Yanking Mr. Gress away from the wall, you push him in the direction of his fellow Freedom Flighters just as the tank comes crashing through the building with its gun aimed right at you.

"To the back exit, quickly!" you shout over the near-deafening sound of falling bricks and plaster.

But it is too late to escape. Two armed men enter from the back room, and two others crawl in from the hole made by the tank. You are surrounded.

58

Even more astonishing is the nature of your attackers. They are all masked and dressed in the green uniforms of HYDRA, an international criminal organization dedicated to world conquest. *What does HYDRA have to do with all this?* you wonder.

A HYDRA commander steps forward brandishing his rifle menacingly. "So . . . Captain America, Freedom Flight—you all are prisoners of HYDRA. Where is she?" he barks.

"Who?" Mr. Gress asks, obviously confused.

"Don't act stupid! Viper—where is she? We know she's here, Gress—her, her rocket, and your five grand. Hand them over immediately."

"I don't know what you're talking about," Gress replies, looking clearly bewildered.

The HYDRA leader knocks Mr. Gress back with the butt of his rifle. "Don't make me angry. I shoot people when I'm angry."

"Be reasonable," you tell the HYDRA leader. "Would they be conducting an illegal purchase in front of me?"

The HYDRA leader does not stop to think about that. Instead he answers, "You, Captain America, you would shield her, thinking your stupid legal system could deal with her. We will deal with her. HYDRA will punish her." The pitch of the man's voice goes up an octave. He sounds hysterical.

"For what?"

"For robbing us," the HYDRA leader shouts, "and trying to incite violence in our territory. The woman is mad, you know."

You nod, but refrain from adding that the HYDRA leader doesn't seem the least bit sane, either.

"If you don't turn her over immediately, I'm going to shoot someone!" the commander screeches.

"But she isn't here," you insist.

"You're lying!"

"Just a minute," one of the other HYDRA agents says. "I think Cap's right. These people wouldn't be buying weapons from Viper right under his nose, would they?"

The HYDRA agents all stare in astonishment at the agent who just spoke. Before they can react further, you grab the HYDRA agent nearest you and send him sprawling back through the hole in the wall. When you look up, you find that the HYDRA agent who took your side has taken out his own partner with a rifle butt.

Unfortunately, the HYDRA leader has Mr. Gress up against the wall and is aiming his rifle at the leader's midsection.

"I knew you were a double agent, Hoffman!" the HYDRA leader screams at the other HYDRA agent. "I loaded your rifle with blanks. Now, don't move, or I'll shoot this fool and then all of you."

From the wild way your attacker is swinging his rifle about, you suspect that he may shoot someone anyway. You must act quickly to get him out of the action. If you want to try to take him out with a flying kick, turn to **180**. If you think you'd be better off trying to grab at him and his gun, turn to **16**.

63 Your shield catches the guard on the side of the head, and he collapses in a dizzy spin. The other guard raises his weapon in your direction, but Agent Bronder

surprises him by squirting him in the face with the selt-
zer hose from behind the bar.

Jumping over the bar, you lay the guard out next to
his friend with a quick right cross. Agent Bronder grabs
his rifle as you retrieve your shield.

Make a Reason FEAT by rolling one die and adding
the result to your Reason ability. If the total is 5 or less,
move to **118**. If it is 6 or better, turn to **10**.

"Sorry. Gotta run," you joke to your unappre- **64**
ciative mechanical opponent as you tuck your body
into a roll, preparing to somersault past it. It fails to
respond to your humor.

Make an Agility FEAT by rolling one die and adding
the result to your Agility ability. If the total is 10 or less,
turn to **138**. If it's 11 or more, turn to **112**.

For several moments you fight a growing dark- **65**
ness. *These two kids are counting on me. I can't pass
out now.*

Finally your vision clears and you are able to draw a
full breath of air. Too late! While Agent Bronder's full
attention is on scooping Nitro's gaseous form into her
vacuum cleaner, Blacklash has taken aim at her back
with his whip.

Turn to **130**.

Viper jerks a dart out from her weapon's belt. **66**
You know she keeps these tiny missiles coated with
lethal snake venom! As she prepares to jab you with the
weapon, you roll away and grab up your shield from
the floor beside you. The dart smashes harmlessly
against the adamantium disk.

"I have to put an end to these tricks," you resolve.
Make a Fighting FEAT by rolling one die and adding the
result to your Fighting skill. If the total is 13 or less,
move on to **163**. If it is 14 or more, turn to **84**.

67 Something about the voice of your anonymous caller is very familiar.

"Look, ya gotta trust me. It isn't a trap or anything," the man's voice whines, and suddenly you know exactly who he is.

"It had better not be, Constrictor," you reply, for the caller is none other than Frank Schlichting, alias the Constrictor, a dangerous super villain you have fought with before.

But there have also been a few occasions when Constrictor has helped you—though usually for his own selfish reasons.

"Sheesh, what are you? Psychic? Did you have to say my name?" Constrictor complains. "Suppose someone's tapped the phone?"

"Keep cool, Constrictor," you urge. "If someone tried that, I'd know. Now, suppose you tell me what this is all about?"

"I don't know all that much about it—but *she's* involved in it."

"Who?"

"Her. Viper." Schlichting whispers as though he's afraid someone will overhear him on his end of the line.

You can't blame him for being afraid. "Viper?" you echo the name in a whisper yourself. A shiver races up your spine, for the Viper is one of your most deadly and vicious enemies. Obsessed with power, she has become an international terrorist determined to destroy the United States.

"Yeah, Viper," the hood repeats. "I'm only telling you because I know she's crazy and someone's gotta stop her.

"What's she up to?" you query.

"I don't know exactly. I only know something's gonna happen at that warehouse tonight. Something about the rocket's red glare. Don't ask me what that means, 'cause I don't know. Just stop her."

"How do you know about the warehouse?"

"I'll have to take the fifth on that question. Trust me, huh?"

"Where can I reach you?" you sigh.

"Don't bother trying. I'm taking a trip—far, far away. If she finds out I got you onto her, I'm dead meat. Good luck, Flagman."

There is a click on the phone as your informant hangs up.

"I suppose there's a chance Constrictor is on the level. Better safe than sorry," you say with a sigh, "especially where Viper's concerned."

Turn to **14**.

You grab at the HYDRA leader's rifle, but his **68** grip is too strong. He manages to turn the gun toward you and fire.

Pain shoots through your leg as your opponent pushes you back out of his way. Subtract 2 from your Health points.

Thinking of the civilians you must protect, you fight the feeling of shock sweeping over your body. You must make an Endurance FEAT by rolling one die and adding the result to your Endurance. If the total is 8 or less, turn to **75**. If it is 9 or more, move on to **207**.

Agent Bronder fires her own rifle over the head **69** of the HYDRA fledgling who tried shooting you from the other tank. He ducks back inside the tank.

"Better stay in there!" Bronder shouts.

Agent Hoffman finishes his own sparring partner off, tossing him into the side of a tank. He takes hold of Commander Wright while you remove your Turtle costume, revealing your true uniform and making it possible for you to retrieve your shield.

"Why'd it take you so long to polish off that one?" Bronder teases her partner.

"He was tough," retorts Hoffman. "What are you still doing on the ground?"

"I sort of wrenched my ankle a little."

"That was pretty stupid."

"Not as stupid as the two guys in that tank trying to make a get away," Bronder sighs, pointing to one of the tanks as it rumbles toward the unopen garage door.

"They don't move very fast, do they," you note wryly.

"Oh, look," Bronder laughs as the other tank starts following. "Their pals have got the same idea."

"Better give SHIELD a call from the minibus," you suggest to Agent Hoffman.

"Where should I tell them they're heading?"

"I don't think they know," Laura snickers. "We've captured the only three HYDRA agents who were familiar with the mission or how to run the tanks for that matter."

"Maybe I should stop them before they cause any damage, or hurt themselves," you say.

"No! Look! They've discovered reverse," Bronder gasps as the first tank backs up into the one behind it. The treads lock against one another.

Once you and the SHIELD agents have exhausted a chuckle from their predicament, you send Agent Hoffman to call SHIELD, while you tie up the three HYDRA officers.

The hatch of one of the tanks opens and a head peeks out. Agent Bronder fires another warning shot, shouting, "You stay in your room until we say you can come out." The hatch closes immediately.

"They may figure out how to operate those cannons," you say.

"That would be interesting," Bronder comments.

You help Bronder into the minibus and then load your prisoners aboard. Agent Hoffman pulls the minibus out of the warehouse just as SHIELD arrives. Add 3 to your Karma points for "capturing" the tanks from HYDRA and keeping them from attacking Freedom Flight.

The SHIELD reinforcements, under the direction of Nick Fury, take charge of the tanks and your prisoners when they arrive.

"You were right about the HYDRA commander," he tells you after interrogating the prisoners. "He knew the Viper's hideout all right, and he cracked like a nut. Apparently he's been under a lot of pressure to capture the Viper."

"Considering what usually happens to HYDRA agents who fail," you reply, "that's understandable."

"Yes. Ironically, he wouldn't have caught her here today anyway. She wasn't at the Freedom Flight's Philadelphia headquarters, she was at their old headquarters on Staten Island. Blacklash was with her, and he got shot by Aaron Gress of Freedom Flight—the guy lost his cool when Viper wouldn't sell him a rocket on credit. Blacklash is in intensive care."

"But Viper escaped?" you ask.

Fury nods. "And we're afraid she may be considering moving her base, in case Blacklash wakes up and talks. But we know where she is if we hurry."

"Where's that?"

"Someplace you already know. Her secret base is a complex hidden beneath the Incline in Pittsburgh, Pennsylvania. You fought there with the Avengers, I believe."

"Yes. It will be good to see the place again, under the circumstances."

"Well, then, let's get to the airport pronto," Nick suggests.

Turn to **40**.

Like a mechanical Grim Reaper, the robot **70** moves forward, its curved-blade arms thrashing back and forth, threatening to cut down anything or anyone in its path. Since the other three Avengers are all able to fly, you realize that you alone are vulnerable to this monster's attacks.

Tearing your eyes away from the robot's weaponry of

hacking machetes, twisting daggers, jabbing spears, and slashing swords, you concentrate instead on the robot's feet. *Those just might be its Achilles' heel, so to speak*, you think, noting that the robot's feet move just as a person's would, but without the protection of flesh about the ankles.

If I can just break the joint or jam something into it, you think, *I may be able to immobilize the robot without damaging it too severely*. The only thing you have at hand to jam the robot's ankle is your shield, and you know that getting your shield back after tossing it close to the floor will be a tricky maneuver, but if you believe it will prove successful, turn to **41**. If you want to try throwing your shield higher so you will be more likely to catch it on the rebound, turn to **182**.

71 You are still a little dazed, and your reflexes are unable to compensate for a sudden movement away from the terminal that Viper makes. Your shield misses her by inches, but smashes into the computer terminal, sending sparks flying.

Viper gasps and whirls around, firing a hand laser pistol at you! An explosive sensation covers your chest as the weapon's beam sears through your costume and armor. You must subtract 6 from your Health points.

If you are out of Health points, your adventure ends here.

If you are still healthy enough to go on, turn to **213**.

72 *I wonder why this basement is so small . . . unless Freedom Flight's members really were frightened of Latverian secret police, if there is such a thing*, you think. *In which case, they may have had some sort of a secret escape exit.*

Searching along the walls of the basement for some structural peculiarity that would indicate a secret panel, you spy a portion of the wall that does not meet the floor. A draft blows out from behind the wall.

What have we here? you wonder. Feeling along the bricks, you discover one that is loose. Pushing it causes a section of the wall to swing back.

"Freeze!" a female voice shouts from the other side of the secret door.

Peering into the darkness beyond, you can discern the figure of a man and a woman, both with pistols aimed at you.

"Laura!" the man says urgently, lowering his gun and pushing his partner's down. "It's Captain America."

The man flicks a light switch to reveal a room furnished with a desk, chair, and cot. A phone sits on the desk. There is a closed door in the back of the room.

"Well, he looked like Blacklash through that tiny peephole," the woman squeaks, offended.

"Blacklash has a ponytail crest on his helmet, and he doesn't carry a shield," the man chides.

"At least I know the difference between Latveria and Latvia," the woman mutters, sinking onto the cot.

"Excuse me," you interrupt, "but you seem to have me at a disadvantage."

"Oh, I'm sorry," the man responds. He hands you an ID folder. "Ken Hoffman, SHIELD. This is my partner, Laura Bronder."

"Pleased to meet you," you answer.

"I was so sure he was Blacklash," Agent Bronder mopes.

"What are you doing here?" you ask.

"I imagine the same thing you're doing—checking out leads on the Viper," Agent Hoffman says. "Colonel Fury said you'd been involved in the Curtis Warehouse affair."

"Nick Fury certainly is well informed," you note, marveling at the efficiency of the director of SHIELD, who is a long-time friend and associate.

"We caught Nitro this morning. He told us he ran into you last night," Hoffman explains. "Apparently he got fed up with working for Viper and quit her. She didn't trust him with any information, though. He didn't even know the location of her hideout, but he claims he eavesdropped on a conversation she had with Black-lash. Supposedly, Viper's meeting someone in this secret complex tomorrow to sell them a rocket."

"Yes, it fits," you say, nodding. "But where is she getting these rockets?"

"She hijacked them from Uncle Sam," Hoffman explains. "Six hundred of them. She's selling them to all sorts of people—as long as they have a grudge that's political in nature."

"She'll start a civil war!" you exclaim.

"Several," Agent Bronder mutters.

"And no doubt scrabble for power in the ensuing chaos," you guess.

"You know her methods well," Hoffman comments.

"Unfortunately, yes," you reply.

Suddenly, the phone on the desk rings. Without hesitation, you answer it. "Hello."

"Good morning, Mr. Gress," a female voice greets you. You recognize the voice immediately. It's Viper!

"I trust," the woman on the other end continues, "that last night's demonstration was sufficient to convince your people that they were in need of the greater protection one of my rockets can afford you."

"Quite," you reply tersely to disguise your voice.

"You have the money?"

"Yes."

"Then I'll be there in ten minutes."

"I need more time," you argue.

"Look, I haven't time for games. If you want the rocket, be there, alone, with the five grand."

Turn to **190**.

Blacklash's whip isn't your only problem now. **73**
Behind you, you can hear Nitro approaching. *I can't
take on both of them at once. I must try to finish off
Blacklash. If I engage him hand-to-hand, close up, his
whips will be less effective.*

With a running leap, you launch yourself at Blacklash. To summon the power to charge him successfully,
make an Endurance FEAT. Roll one die and add the
result to your Endurance ability. If the total is 9 or less,
turn to **83**. If it is 10 or more, proceed to **142**.

Summoning a burst of strength, you grab for **74**
Agent Bronder's hand and scramble up the ladder. You
strap yourself in as the SHIELD agent lifts the helicopter off the roof of HYDRA's secret base.

Using one hand to pilot the craft, she presses a clean
handkerchief against your shoulder wound.

"I can get that," you say holding the makeshift bandage tight.

"You okay?" she asks.

"Just fine," you declare.

Turn to **89**.

You are losing your battle against the shock **75**
caused by your wound, but just as you begin to black
out, you notice with relief that the HYDRA commander
is fleeing the room.

When you come to, you are in a more familiar place—
a private hospital room in SHIELD headquarters. Hovering over you is the anxious face of Nick Fury, the
director of SHIELD.

"You gave us quite a scare there, Mister." The gruff,
former Army colonel smiles. "How are you feeling?"

"A little groggy," you admit. "I guess I'm not as invul-
nerable as I thought."

"The doctors say you'll be up in no time—on
crutches for a few weeks, but up in no time," Fury says,
trying to cheer you.

"That double agent working with HYDRA? Was he a SHIELD agent? What was he doing at Freedom Flight headquarters?" You have more questions than you can ask in one breath.

Fury sits down next to you. "Yeah, Hoffman is one of my boys. He was working undercover. We'd heard a rumor that HYDRA knew Viper's whereabouts. We've been trying to locate Viper ever since she stole the shipment of rockets that she's been trying to sell. HYDRA won't tell us anything because they want to deal with her themselves and get hold of the rockets."

"But Viper wasn't at Freedom Flight," you note, puzzled.

"No. But they thought she would be. Evidently they'd tapped into Viper's phone lines and heard a Mr. Gress arranging to meet her this morning."

"That must have been the other Mr. Gress—Kurt Gress's cousin Aaron Gress—at the old headquarters on Staten Island," you surmise.

"Yes. That's what we figured out. When we interrogated Nitro this morning, he clued us in on the fact that Viper was selling a rocket there. Nitro had run off from Viper because he didn't like taking orders from her. But he couldn't tell us anything about her headquarters. He claims he never really knew where it was because he only came and went via her teleporter."

"So what happened at the real rendezvous site?" you ask.

"Well, we got there a little late. Viper was gone. Aaron

70

Gress lost his temper when Viper wouldn't sell him a rocket on credit, so Blacklash got rough, but Gress had a gun hidden on him and shot the hoodlum. Viper left Blacklash behind. He's in intensive care now. By the time he wakes up to talk, Viper'll probably be gone. We confiscated the rocket, but the HYDRA leader who shot you escaped, so now we have no leads on Viper."

"I'm sorry, Nick."

"It's not your fault. You saved a lot of lives today. Besides that, you've inspired a new public relations team to help combat Viper's schemes."

"I don't understand."

"According to Aaron Gress, Viper was selling these rockets real cheap. So money was not her motivation. We suspect she wanted to stir up trouble among all the different political groups in the country."

"And try to take over in the ensuing violence and chaos. Typical. So how have I inspired this PR team?"

"Well, if you feel up to visitors, I'll show you." Nick Fury ushers two men into your room—Kurt Gress of Freedom Flight and Steven Curtis of People's Choice of Latveria.

"Have you two settled your differences?" you ask in surprise.

"Well, no," Mr. Gress admits. "I still think Victor Von Doom is a tyrant—"

"You want another corrupt puppet like King Zorba?" Mr. Curtis snarls.

"PLEASE, gentlemen," Nick Fury breaks in to remind them, "you were supposed to give Cap the *good* news."

"Sorry," Mr. Curtis mutters.

"Excuse me," Mr. Gress says. "What we meant to say is that we don't hold each other responsible for the rocket incidents, and that even though we disagree, we will not allow ourselves to be manipulated by this Viper woman into using violence against one another."

"Yes," Mr. Curtis agrees. "And we are going to give a press conference together to warn other political groups about her."

71

"Thank you, both of you." You smile. "That will be a great help."

"We have to leave now," Mr. Gress announces. "We're filming our announcement for the evening news at the Balch Institute."

"What's that?" you ask.

"It's sort of a museum celebrating the variety of ethnic cultures that have contributed their heritage to America," Mr. Gress explains.

"And their different ideas? Very appropriate," you say. "Good luck."

After the two men leave, you turn again to Nick Fury. "It looks like we've lost the Viper, though."

"But if others listen to Curtis and Gress," Fury replies, "we may just file her fangs down a bit."

"Let's hope so," you agree.

Your adventure is over. You may begin again, subtracting 1 point from your initial Health total and 1 point from your Karma for losing Viper.

76 Your new phony super-villain costume is green like those of HYDRA's minions, with a large pocket in the back of the shirt, where you can hide your shield.

"You can tell them it's armor to protect you from being shot in the back," Agent Hoffman suggests, tapping on the hump your shield makes on your back.

"I feel a little like a turtle," you admit.

"The Sinister Turtle," Agent Bronder jokingly dubs you.

"Once you impress HYDRA with your fighting, they

won't care if your name is Dr. Seuss," Nick Fury comments. "Just be sure you don't impress them too much or they're liable to get suspicious."

You and Agents Bronder and Hoffman take a taxi to a large, supposedly abandoned, warehouse where the HYDRA recruitment tryouts are being held. In the center of the warehouse are a few mats where all muscles-for-hire must go a round against some HYDRA goon to demonstrate their fighting skills. Exactly as Nick Fury suggested, you refrain from showing off all your talent. Nonetheless, you manage to impress the HYDRA agents who are judging the battles.

After you've had your turn, you watch Agents Hoffman and Bronder take theirs. You can tell they've both trained under Nick Fury and learned a lot from him. Like you, they must hold back some to keep from looking too good. They join you when they are finished.

A HYDRA agent with a clipboard walks up to you. "You three together?" he asks.

"Depends," you reply. Fury's orders were that neither of his agents was to take the assignment alone, but if only two of you were chosen, the mission would continue.

"Hmm," is the HYDRA agent's response. "You two guys are in," he says, pointing to you and Hoffman. "You ever type on a computer, honey?" he asks Agent Bronder.

"I want to fight," Bronder says through clenched teeth.

"Look, hon, data entry pays just about the same, and it's a lot safer. Take it or leave it."

Agent Bronder's face clouds over with annoyance, but just as the HYDRA agent is ready to walk away, Bronder says in a disappointed tone, "I'll take it."

"Good decision, come with me. You two guys, get in that truck by the loading dock."

"She didn't look too happy," you say, looking at Agent Hoffman.

"I know. She's a great actress," Hoffman says quietly. "What a lucky break. This way we won't have to sneak

73

into HYDRA's computer complex."

"You really think she'll be able to locate Viper's base from HYDRA's computer? HYDRA's technology is extremely advanced," you point out.

"Laura could make a computer sit up and beg. She'll find it."

"Then it will be up to us to see that she gets out safely," you reply.

HYDRA locks you, Hoffman, and all the other hirelings in a windowless truck trailer and drives all of you to their own secret headquarters. You can tell you are headed roughly south, deeper into New Jersey, but you can't get a better fix on your position, even after the truck doors are finally opened, because you are in an underground garage.

"Gee, Toto," Agent Hoffman jokes in a whispered voice, "this doesn't look like Fort Dix."

"No, but we can't be too far away from it," you reply, marveling at the arrogance HYDRA must possess to station themselves so near a U.S. Army base. You nudge Hoffman and indicate with a nod of your head a windowless minibus from which seven women, including Agent Bronder, are debarking.

"The gang's all here," Hoffman mutters.

You and Agent Hoffman spend the rest of the day training in HYDRA's private little army gymnasiums without windows. The exercises are grueling and repetitive, but nothing you aren't used to.

Finally, an announcement is made that the work day is over. After assigning you to a dorm room and giving you a chance to clean up, HYDRA guards lead you to several large adjoining lounges. Within, there are bars serving free drinks, and banquet tables covered with food. Rock music is piped into some of the lounges for dancing, while there are televisions, pool tables, and video games in others. You notice some women already inside.

"Ah, the wages of sin," Agent Hoffman murmurs for your hearing alone. "I'm going to rush the food—I'm starving. Coming?"

74

"Grab me one of those corned beef sandwiches; I'm going to look for Laura," you answer.

It takes you a while, milling through the press of people, but you finally spot Agent Bronder surrounded by some of your fellow hired thugs.

"Yoo-hoo, Turtle," she calls out, managing to push through her would-be suitors to your side and look charmingly up at you.

You hear one of them mutter, "What is it about those costumed types that attracts dames so much?"

"Where's Ken?" Agent Bronder asks.

"Eating," you reply.

"Figures," Bronder sniffs.

"We had a long hard day. A man needs something to keep up his strength."

Hanging on your arm and keeping her voice low, she says, "Well, I've been cracking through top-secret data banks all day, and the thought of food right now turns my stomach. D'you know they have a file on you 420 pages long?"

"I suppose I should be honored."

"I just don't understand it. The computer's given me the names of half the honchos in charge of this operation, but I can't get a single line on Viper."

Make a Reason FEAT by rolling one die and adding the result to your Reason ability. If the total is 5 or less, turn to **151**. If it is 6 or more, go to **56**.

Once you are outside the Avengers Mansion, **77** you climb wearily onto your customized Harley-Davidson motorcycle. Your wound still smarts.

You cycle through town until dusk, but nothing unusual comes to your attention. Nothing nags at you but the pain of your wound. Finally, at the end of the day, after you've pulled your Harley-Davidson into your customized van parked behind Avengers Mansion, you remove your helmet and collapse, exhausted, onto the built-in cot. "I'll only lie here for a minute," you assure yourself.

Make an Endurance FEAT. Roll one die and add the result to your Endurance ability. If the total is 8 or less, turn to **209**. If it is 9 or more, turn to **99**.

Laura Bronder's face falls and Ken Hoffman **78** looks clearly worried when you decline their assistance, but they escort you to the mine entrance you have chosen, and wish you luck before they head back to their own stations.

It takes a while for your eyes to adjust to the dim beam of the flashlight after being out in the sunshine, but with a photocopy of Agent Lamb's map you proceed through the mine tunnels swiftly enough.

Agent Lamb's doubts about his map's accuracy are well founded. You come to an unmentioned place where the floor drops away in an unmarked shaft down. The hole cannot be skirted, so you back up to get a running start to leap over it. Make a Strength FEAT to leap across the hole. If your total is 8 or less, turn to **149**. If it is 9 or more, turn to **46**.

Your shield slams into Viper, and she crumbles **79** to the ground. You leap to her side and bend over her, seeking to recover her teleport ring before she revives. Once you get that off her finger, you begin disarming her.

Just as you are unbuckling the villainess's weapon belt, Agent Bronder screams your name from the next room.

Grabbing your shield, you dash in to discover Agent Bronder pinned under the artificial force generated by Blacklash's gravity bolo, and unable to aid her partner. Across the room, Blacklash has Hoffman wrapped in a necro-lash, a special whip through which Blacklash can channel a deadly jolt of electricity. On seeing you, however, the super criminal lets go of this weapon, allowing his victim's body to collapse on the floor. With lightning speed, Blacklash reaches for a second metal whip that he has converted into nunchakus—oriental battle-staves.

"Blacklash," you growl, "if you think you're going to stop me with those sticks, you're sadly mistaken."

You charge for your foe. Make an Endurance FEAT by rolling one die and adding the result to your Endurance ability. If the total is 8 or less, turn to **187**, if it is 9 or more, go to **94**.

80 Your shield lodges perfectly in the ankle joint of your mechanical opponent, but the robot takes another step toward you, and a machete slashes within an inch of your chest.

You are ready to leap to avoid a blood bath when there is a terrible screeching sound as the robot's foot shears off of the pin holding its leg. The robot loses its balance and keels over helplessly. Your shield pops out of the broken joint like a slice of bread from a toaster.

Thor's hammer couldn't have returned more smoothly, you think, smirking with satisfaction as you catch the disk.

Add 2 Karma points to your total and turn to **178**.

81 You catch the guard in a headlock, but your hold is not tight enough to keep him from jabbing you in the leg with his weapon—a stun gun that delivers a strong electric shock. You must subtract 2 from your Health points.

You are paralyzed momentarily, but Agent Hoffman kicks the weapon from the guard's hand before he can use it again.

"Come on, Laura!" Hoffman shouts to his partner. "We haven't got all day."

Agent Bronder gives the last HYDRA recruit a shove backward and hops out of the bus. You and Agent Hoffman climb out behind her, forcing the HYDRA guard to come with you.

Turn to **32**.

You tackle Nitro hard and he goes over the edge **82** of the loading dock, with you right on top of him. When you get up, he does not.

Nudging the unconscious exploding man with her toe, Agent Bronder sighs, "Now I'll never know if my Nitro-buster works."

Just as she stoops down to check Nitro's pulse and breathing, you see that Blacklash has crept up on the two of you and is now aiming one of his steel whips at the SHIELD agent's back!

"Look out!" you warn, grabbing the woman and shoving her out of range of the whip that comes slashing down where she stood only a moment ago. The weapon raises sparks along the pavement, and Blacklash closes in on the two of you, a whip poised in each of his hands.

"I've been waiting for this rematch, Captain America," the villain says.

"Love to lose, don't you, Blacklash," you taunt as you whip your shield in his direction. Make a Shield FEAT by rolling one die and adding the result to your Shield ability. If the total is 18 or less, turn to **98**, if it is 19 or greater, turn to **170**.

Though you knock into Blacklash, you only **83** succeed in pushing him back several yards, and now you are in even better range of his whips. One of them cracks painfully across your knees. Subtract 6 from your Health point total.

Apparently impatient to finish you off, Blacklash retracts his whips and approaches you with his gravity bola—a weapon with an artificial gravity field that could easily drag you to the ground if its owner manages to entangle you in it.

Worse, Nitro is right behind you. *Probably thinks he's sneaked up on me, though I could hear him across the yard. I've got to time this just right,* you think.

Make an Agility FEAT by rolling one die and adding the result to your Agility ability. If the total is 12 or less, turn to **34**. If it's 13 or more, move on to **188**.

84 This is no time to treat a lady kindly. You land a right cross on Viper's chin and she slumps to the ground. Quickly, you remove her teleporter ring so she can't get away.

Turn to **215**.

85 You launch yourself feet first at the HYDRA leader, but he too is skilled at combat. In one smooth movement, he ducks and twirls around, firing at you with his rifle. You know you've been hit as you crash to the floor in pain. Subtract 4 from your Health points.

If you have 10 or more Health points, move on **207**. If you have fewer than 10 Health points, you must turn to **75**.

86 You can't wrest the rifle from the guard's grip, and he manages to fire the weapon, though it is no longer aimed. A bullet grazes your leg. You must subtract 2 points from your Health.

You are still able to knock the guard off balance, slamming him against the floor by knocking his legs out from under him. He lies still. His partner flops down on top of him, stunned by a karate chop from Agent Bronder. She retrieves the rifle as you pick up your shield.

If your Health has dropped to 0 or less, you are in no shape to continue on, and your adventure ends here.

If you are still okay, turn to **118**.

Your timing is off by just a second, and though **87**
the robot wobbles for a moment, it remains upright and
advances toward you. Catching your shield on the
rebound not a moment too soon, you use it to ward off
the deadly weaponry slashing down on you. You know
that you'd better dodge out of the way before the robot
turns you into hamburger.

Turn to **64.**

You creep toward the Viper with every muscle **88**
tensed. So much depends on capturing her. You think
of all the destruction she has caused, the number of
times she has tried to kill you. . . . A piece of broken
glass crunches beneath your foot.

Viper spins about with her weapon raised. You can
see that it is no ordinary gun, but instead, a deadly
energy-beam generator.

Just at that moment, Blacklash cries out behind you,
no doubt surprised to find that the figure underneath
the ladder is quite active. You hurl your shield in
Viper's direction.

Make a Shield FEAT by rolling one die and adding the
result to your Shield ability. If the total is 18 or less,
turn to **33**. If it is 19 or more, go to **197.**

The night air is exhilarating. You enjoy watch- **89**
ing the lights below you recede into pinpoints. Bronder
holds the copter in a hover for a minute.

"Hadn't you better move away before they give chase
in the other chopper?" you suggest.

"If they try chasing us in that, they'll be landing
quickly and wearing out their Keds running beneath
us," Bronder predicts.

"You know a lot about helicopters?" you ask.

Bronder nods. "Colonel Fury's been training me, but
I've got to confess—I haven't got my pilot's license yet."

"I'll have to slap your wrist after we land," you tease.

Turn to **133.**

90 You are unable to fight Blacklash's weapon. Pinned to the ground by the bola, you are at the mercy of your foes, and they show no mercy. Pummeled ruthlessly by the two villains, you quickly lose consciousness.

You awaken from one nightmare into another. You are bruised and bloodied from the merciless beating you took while you were unable to defend yourself. Whatever your Health points were, they are now at exactly 10.

But the worst part of this too-real nightmare is the face leering over you. With a painful gasp, you recognize the face of your archenemy.

"Viper!" You automatically try to struggle to your feet, but you realize that you are restrained to a table by steel straps.

Viper's attractive face is distorted by a hateful sneer and the shade of green lipstick she wears. "Welcome, Captain America," she laughs. "I must admit, I am impressed. My plan is only in its initial stages, and already you've stuck your shield in where it doesn't belong. However do you do it?"

You pull yourself together enough to speak, hoping that your bravado will encourage Viper to become careless so you can learn her scheme and be better prepared if you can escape. "Still as mad as ever, Viper? Playing with rockets now, are we?"

"Not exactly, Captain. I let others play with the rockets. My role is simply to sell them. What I want to know is how you found out where we'd be operating from last night."

"A little birdie told me," you reply, determined not to give up your source and put him in danger.

Viper sneers. "We'll find out eventually, my red, white, and black and 'blue prisoner. We'll find out everything you know about our plan. Then we'll make you part of it. Won't that be amusing? Captain America helping to destroy his own country!"

"Your schemes have always failed in the past, Viper," you retort.

"Ah, but this time I'm going to let America destroy itself. Then you will see how dangerous your precious liberty and justice for all can be."

"You're babbling, Viper," you taunt.

"Am I? We shall see."

You shudder as Viper leaves the room. Turn to **191**.

91 It only takes you a few hours to drive down to Philadelphia, but by the time you arrive, Frank Schlichting, alias the Constrictor, has already checked out of the Liberty Hotel.

The hotel clerk tells you he left in a big hurry looking frightened, but he paid his bill.

"Frightened of whom, I wonder?" you say aloud. And then think to yourself, *I should check out Freedom Flight while I'm down here. If Viper tried to sell a rocket to the PLC, she may have tried to sell one to Freedom Flight, too.*

Since Freedom Flight's new headquarters keeps regular business hours, you will have to wait until morning to check them out. You spend the night sleeping in your van. Add 1 back to your Health points. Turn to **62**.

92 "Let me see that wound," Agent Hoffman demands, pressing a clean handkerchief against your flesh to stop the bleeding.

One of your former prisoners hands him a first-aid kit, and in a few minutes the SHIELD agent has bandaged you expertly. Add 1 to your Health points.

"Looks good. Thanks," you say.

"You're very welcome," says Hoffman.

Turn to **147**.

93 Your shield bounces off the robot's chest with a resounding clank and lands some distance behind you. Undamaged, the robot closes in on you, and the tips of its two machete arms slash through your costume, scraping against the steel mesh tunic you wear beneath it.

You make a quick backward dive toward your shield as a spear releases from your foe's arsenal and hurls toward you. With a quick roll, you manage to avoid the full impact of the weapon, but it shaves a layer each of your costume and skin from your arm.

Subtract 5 from your Health points. You may not subtract any of this damage from your Karma.

The robot proceeds to close in on you menacingly, but a flash of light streaks toward it and then through it. Captain Marvel appears over you. "You all right, Cap?" she inquires. Behind her, you can see the robot spinning about in confusion, its command signals no doubt scrambled by your partner.

"Just a flesh wound to the arm and a blow to my pride," you answer, picking up your shield as you stand up. Turn to **175**.

The force of your attack knocks Blacklash to **94** the ground, nearly on top of Agent Bronder. As you struggle to pin the villain's arms down so he cannot activate his teleporter ring, you hear a hissing noise by your side. Blacklash ceases his struggles and goes limp.

Still entangled in the bolo, Agent Bronder withdraws an automatic hypodermic from Blacklash's arm and pulls the criminal's teleporter ring from his finger.

"Good work," you compliment her, lifting the gravity bolo off her and leaving it over Blacklash.

"Hey, down, but never out," she smiles. She moves immediately to her partner's side. "Ken, are you okay?" she asks loudly, giving him a shake.

"Not now, Melanie," Hoffman mutters.

"He'll be fine," Bronder announces.

"Who's Melanie?" you ask.

"I'm sure I wouldn't know," Agent Bronder sniffs. Suddenly she freezes. "Did you close Viper up in there?" she asks, pointing to the door to the smaller room, which is now shut.

"No. She must have come to." You turn the doorknob, but the door won't budge.

"She's barricaded herself in," Bronder says, smiling. "I jammed that other door but good. What's she going to do, now? Dig her way out?"

A muffled explosion reaches your ears. "She must have had something hidden in her boot," you guess. "She's probably made another hole to escape through."

Agent Bronder helps shove on the door, but it doesn't budge an inch.

"This is useless."

The two of you rush for the metal ladder and climb out through the manhole, but by the time you reach the street, there is no sign of your prey.

Several SHIELD vehicles pull up in front of you, and Agent Bronder orders some of them to start patrolling for Viper. "We each still have a teleporter ring," she points out. "Want to take a little trip?"

"Much too dangerous, young lady," says a familiar voice from behind.

Turning around, you recognize Nick Fury, director of SHIELD. "I agree. Viper would have an ambush waiting for anyone foolish enough to try," you add.

"I thought our paths would cross," Fury says as he shakes your hand. "Would you hand the rings over to Dr. Arney—quickly please," he says, pointing to a man in white lab coat waiting at the door to a van loaded with electronic equipment.

You hand your ring to the scientist. Bronder does too, though somewhat reluctantly.

"I just saw HYDRA drag Viper into one of their jet-copters, but I couldn't catch up to them. With any luck, Dr. Arney will be able to trace a signal from one of those rings, and we'll discover Viper's headquarters before HYDRA makes a deal with her," Fury informs both of you.

"HYDRA?" you ask. "What do they have to do with this?"

"Well," Nick Fury explains, "being an international crime syndicate that is more than casually interested in world conquest, HYDRA was after the same rockets Viper stole. They've been swearing they'd get even with her, and now she's their prisoner. She's in more trouble than she bargained for."

"Got it, Colonel," Dr. Arney calls out. "Pittsburgh. The computer has the exact coordinates. Shall I relay the information to the local authorities?"

"Yes," Fury answers. "With both Viper and Blacklash out of the way, taking her hideout shouldn't be too difficult. Thanks for your help, Cap."

"Yes," Agent Bronder echoes. "You were great."

"You're both very welcome," you answer. "I'm just relieved that this rocket scam didn't get any further out of hand. Please remember, you can count on me when Viper gets out of HYDRA's clutches and starts hatching another scheme."

Your adventure is over. You may begin a new adventure, adding 1 to your initial Karma for having stopped Viper—if only for the time being.

After binding your ankle tightly, you use your **95** shield to create dents in the wall so you can try to climb out. But the pain from your injury makes climbing and balancing exceedingly difficult.

After attempting the cliff-like walls and falling from them three separate times, you realize it will take more energy than you are able to summon, and even if you succeeded, you would have no strength left to battle the Viper anyway. You sit down to wait. Turn to **168**.

I don't want to risk losing my shield just yet. I **96** *may need it.*

To sneak up on Blacklash, make an Intuition FEAT by rolling one die and adding the result to your Intuition ability. If the total is 10 or less, turn to **60**. If it's 11 or more, turn to **211**.

Your blow knocks the HYDRA commander **97** down, and his rifle clatters across the floor. One of the prisoners has the presence of mind to pick it up and

87

hold it on his former captor. Add 2 to your Karma points for defeating the HYDRA commander.

You watch as Agent Hoffman polishes off the only other HYDRA guard in the room by tossing him out through the hole in the wall made by the tank.

Turn to **123**.

98 Blacklash deflects your shield at the last moment by converting one of his whips into improvised nunchaku—oriental battle staves—and then smacking the disk aside.

Agent Hoffman comes running out of the shadows and tackles the villain before he can smack his whip down on you. Blacklash manages to tumble away from the SHIELD agent, however, and a strange glow encompasses him. A moment later, the villain has disappeared.

Turn to **26**.

99 You rouse yourself with a start just before you fall asleep. After attaching the portable computer terminal hidden in the bottom of your briefcase to the phone-link computer interface built into the van, you key in your access code. In a moment, you are connected to the computer that answers calls to your nationwide hot line. The calls have been presorted for you by a volunteer staff of amateur computer operators who call themselves Stars and Stripes.

On the head of the list is a message that has been left

four times—at fifteen, sixteen, seventeen, and eighteen hundred hours. The computer printout of the message reads, "I must speak with you personally, not with this machine. I'll call back in exactly one hour."

Checking your watch, you learn that it is nearly nineteen hundred hours. Quickly you punch in a code number that will allow you to listen in on and, if you desire, speak with, anyone calling the hot-line number.

Exactly on the hour, someone calls and starts to deliver the same message to the computer recorder.

It's a man's voice. Breaking in on it, you announce, "This is Captain America, not a recording. How can I help you?"

"It's about time!" the caller replies rudely. "You gotta be at Curtis Supply Warehouse in Newark at midnight. You may see something of interest."

"If you don't give me more details, I'm not going anywhere," you declare.

Make an Intuition FEAT by rolling one die and adding the result to your Intuition ability. If the total is 10 or less, turn to **185**. If it is 11 or more, turn to **67**.

The passage begins sloping down steadily. **100** Then you spot them. The rockets! There are several hundred lined up in the passage.

Hearing footsteps, you take shelter behind the missiles. Ahead you hear a familiar voice—imperious and harsh—the Viper's voice.

"Keep up the transferences until you are no longer able. Don't you dare stop for a minor thing such as gunfire," the villainess says.

Peeping from your hiding place, you see she is speaking to two underlings struggling under the weight of one of the rockets. As the three figures head down the corridor, you stalk behind them. They come to a junction. The men with the rocket turn left and the Viper goes right.

If you try to stop the men sending the rockets off, you will lose the Viper, and that you do not feel you should risk. If she gets away now, she will still have several rockets available, but if you capture her, she won't be able to use any of them.

At the junction, you fervently wish there were two of you. You must subtract 1 from your Karma points as you allow the men transferring the rockets to continue unchallenged. You follow Viper down the right-hand corridor.

Turn to **173**.

101 You decide to rest the extra day, so you turn in early and get another good night's sleep, which does you a lot of good. Add 2 more to your Health points.

You call the Liberty Hotel in Philadelphia, only to learn that Mr. Schlichting checked out suddenly last night. "I would have missed him even if I'd driven down last night," you console yourself.

You also try ringing Freedom Flight's new Philadelphia headquarters, but no one picks up the phone on the other end. *That's strange,* you think. *Well, at least now I'll get ahead of my sketch deadlines.*

After one more peaceful day at the drawing board, you feel a lot better. Add 4 more back to your Health points.

Toward evening, you are impatient to begin tracking Viper. "I just hope the trail's not cold."

Just as you are about to drive your van down to Philadelphia to see what's going on at Freedom Flight headquarters, your phone rings. It's Nick Fury of SHIELD. "Glad I caught you, Cap. I was afraid you'd be out of town."

"I was just leaving, but I suspect the trail may be cold by now."

"In that case, maybe you'd consider giving us a hand with this Viper thing. We've got a lead that takes us to HYDRA, and we could use someone like you."

"I thought you'd never ask, Nick."

"Great. Meet me here at SHIELD headquarters in one hour."

I wonder what he's found out? you ask yourself, as you head your van back toward New York City. *Well, I'll find out soon enough.* Turn to **198**.

You are startled by a snarl from the Sub- **102** Mariner, and your aim is thrown off by a fraction of an inch. Your shield misses the narrow beam.

Out of the corner of your eye, you can see Namor standing at his team's basket beside your own, still growling and shaking small red flecks from his hand, but you are more concerned with the path of your shield. The disk ricochets off the side wall and hurtles back toward you. There is no time to retrieve it before the energy beam strikes Captain Marvel. Turn to **195**.

Your kick never lands on the commander. **103** Rifle fire aimed at you hits him when you bend to wind up for your karate kick. The commander is knocked off the top of the tank by the force of the bullets, and you follow him down, bullets bouncing off the shield hidden in the back of your costume.

Hidden behind the tank, you can see Commander Wright is dead, shot by one of his own underlings atop the other tank. Now you will never learn if the HYDRA officer knew the location of Viper's secret base.

Turn to **61**.

You grab Blacklash in a full nelson, startling **104** him into dropping his necro-lash before he can injure Agent Hoffman.

"Get his teleporter ring!" you shout. Blacklash struggles futilely as the SHIELD agent yanks at the wide band set with a huge crystal.

With the loss of this escape route, Blacklash's struggling ceases.

After freeing his partner from Blacklash's gravity bolo, Agent Hoffman gives the villain a taste of his own medicine by wrapping him in the powerful weapon.

With Blacklash weighted to the floor, the three of you are free to interrogate him.

"Haven't you got more important things to do than hound me?" the criminal asks you.

"More important, Scarlotti!" you reply in astonishment, addressing Blacklash by his real name. "You don't seem to realize the trouble you've caused, the trouble you're in."

Scarlotti shrugs as well as he can in his predicament. "So I've helped a few kooks blow each other up."

"With rockets stolen from the U.S. Government, scuzball," Agent Bronder snarls.

"Big deal," Blacklash yawns.

"Viper is pushing these rockets for a fraction of their worth, not to mention their black market value. Doesn't that suggest anything to you, Scarlotti?" Agent Hoffman asks.

Blacklash looks at him blankly.

"She's trying to turn this entire nation into a battleground," you explain patiently. "Do you have any idea what that would be like?"

"Don't try to kid me. She hasn't got that many rockets," Blacklash argues.

"She started with six hundred," Hoffman replies.

"Six hundred!" Blacklash snorts, unbelieving. "She told me I'd have to make do with just one to analyze."

"She's very frugal," Agent Hoffman replies.

"So you have been helping her try to copy them, as well?" Bronder asks.

Suddenly nervous, Blacklash turns his head away saying, "I want to talk to my lawyer. And I'm going to tell him you people haven't informed me of my rights yet."

"We'll get you a lawyer, Scarlotti," Hoffman says.

"The only thing is, we haven't decided what we're going to be charging you with yet."

"Terrorism or treason," Bronder adds.

"That's crazy!" Blacklash shouts. "I haven't done either."

"On numerous occasions, Viper has made known her intentions to destroy our nation, of which you are a citizen, Blacklash," you point out. "She's mad. What's your excuse?"

"If I help you, you won't try pinning any of this treason stuff on me?" Blacklash asks.

"Word of honor," Hoffman agrees.

Blacklash looks at you for more assurance.

"We don't want to hound you, Scarlotti," you insist. "We just want Viper. We need to know her secret base, and quickly, before she manages to move it."

"Pittsburgh," Scarlotti answers.

"The one spelled with an 'H,' in Pennsylvania?" Bronder asks.

"Yeah. Under the Incline."

"What's that?" Hoffman asks.

"It's sort of like a cable car," you explain. "It goes up the side of Mount Washington."

"How do you know these things?" Bronder asks, clearly impressed.

"I fought in a battle there before, alongside the Avengers."

"Care to fight a battle there with us, too?" Hoffman asks.

"I'd be honored," you answer.

Turn to 186.

105
To fight the effects of the hypnotic ray, you try to turn your head away from it, but it is as though your skull is held in a vice. Your determination, it seems, may not be enough. In another few moments, the only thing you see on the screen is the serpent stare pattern, indicating that Viper has erased the information on her customer list to keep it from SHIELD.

Coming closer to you, the Viper whispers in your ear, "I'm very sorry I can't take you with me, Captain, but it's too far for my teleporter ring to carry us both. I'll just have to destroy you now."

Unable to struggle, you watch in horror as Viper draws out a throwing dart from her equipment belt. You know she keeps these darts tipped with a deadly snake venom. Viper poises the dart at your throat and then draws it back, preparing to plunge it in deep, but a plasma beam fired right over your shoulder knocks her aside.

A second beam shatters the screen and in a moment you are able to move again. Nick Fury stands beside you, his SHIELD weapon again aimed at Viper.

Recognizing that she is outgunned, the villainess activates her ring and disappears.

"Are you all right, Cap?" Fury asks holstering his weapon.

"Fine," you answer. "Thanks," you add, nodding toward the floor where Viper dropped the venom dart she almost killed you with. "We lost her again."

"Yes, but you distracted her attention from the rockets. Agents Hoffman and Bronder infiltrated her cargo teleporter room and kept any more of them from being transported away."

"But she sold a lot of them, Nick," you reply. "And I couldn't escape the effects of her serpent stare while she erased her list of customers."

"But we recovered the majority. Don't worry. We'll catch up to her eventually," Fury says.

"Undoubtedly. She'll find we aren't so easily crushed," you vow.

Your adventure ends here. You may begin again, subtracting 1 point from your inital Karma for what you have learned.

106 You want to put this mechanical porcupine out of misery, but not destroy it totally. Taking careful aim at the robot's shoulder, you wait for the moment when one of its feet is off the floor, reasoning that this would be the best time to knock it off balance.

To attempt this FEAT, roll one die and add the result to your Shield skill. If the total is 17 or less, turn to **87**. If it is 18 or 19, turn to **57**. If it is 20 or more, turn to **158**.

107 Deciding that what you have to learn is more likely to come from Freedom Flight's members than the burned-out shell of their old headquarters, you climb out of the empty basement. Your drive to Philadelphia takes only a few hours, but Freedom Flight's new headquarters has already shut down for the day.

You spend the evening working on sketches for Marvel Comics, and turn in early. After another night's sleep, you recover a little more from your last battle. Add 2 more points back to your Health.

Turn to **62**.

108 After being briefed by Nick Fury and Agent Hoffman on your HYDRA mission, you get a night's sleep—a restless night's sleep, but better than nothing. Add 1 to your Health points.

Very early the next morning, dressed in a phony super villain costume that hides your shield in the lining of a cape, you show up at a secret HYDRA recruitment center that SHIELD learned about from an informant. Since HYDRA is anxious to hire enough muscle to tackle Viper's secret base, they are not overly particular or careful about who they hire.

You must fight with a few HYDRA agents to prove your skill, just as Agent Hoffman and his partner did two days ago, and then you are sent in a closed truck to a secret location somewhere in New Jersey where you are drilled as though you are a private in a semi-disciplined army.

At the end of the day, just as Agent Hoffman predicted, you are given freedom to roam through the secret base's elaborate entertainment lounges. There you find a free food buffet, numerous bars serving free drinks, dance floors with piped in rock music, giant-screen televisions, video games, and pool tables.

You aren't interested in any of these pleasures, however. Though there aren't many women among the new fighting personnel, it is difficult in the press of bodies to find the one woman you seek.

Taking Fury's suggestion, you stay by the pool tables, and after nearly an hour, you spot your quarry. As she starts racking the balls on her table, you approach her, holding out a piece of jewelry Agent Hoffman gave to you.

"Excuse me, did you drop this, Ms. Bronder?"

She looks up, prepared to give you a withering glance, but she sees what you hold. "My charm bracelet! I thought I left that in—" You can see the look of realization cross her face—that she left it in her locker at SHIELD headquarters and you must have come from there. "—in my room," she finishes. "Thank you."

"You're welcome," you answer.

"You play pool, Mr., er . . ."

"They call me the Ranger," you interject, using the code identity Fury helped you invent to hide your Captain America costume.

"Ranger," she repeats. "Laura," she introduces herself. "I always was a soft touch for masked men," she smiles as she lays the cue ball down and prepares to break.

On the pretext of showing her how to shoot straighter, you lean over her closely, whispering, "Your uncle is furious. He wants you to come home tonight even if you haven't got a present for him."

"I got him a perfectly smashing present," Agent Bronder whispers back. After she sends the billiard balls spinning across the table, she adds, "I just can't get it mailed."

"Well, you're in luck. I deliver twenty-four hours a day."

"Not likely," she whispers, nodding toward the armed guards at every door, "unless you've got a Smith and Wesson full of silver bullets hidden in the folds of that cape."

You shake your head. "Just my star-spangled shield," you whisper back.

Agent Bronder's eyes grow quite wide. She gulps. "I guess my uncle must really care about me."

You stick very close together, mostly shooting pool and dancing until HYDRA's midnight curfew. Then you sneak behind a bar as veteran HYDRA agents begin clearing the room.

You remove the cape and retrieve your shield. "Put this on," you order, handing the SHIELD agent the cape.

"It weighs a ton. Teflon shielding, I presume?"

"Yes. Shh."

You can hear the HYDRA guards patrolling by your hiding place. They are the only ones left in the lounge. After they check all the rooms, they turn out the lights and close and lock the main doors.

"They'll look here again when security doesn't find us in our rooms," Agent Bronder warns.

"We should be long gone by then," you whisper, when the lounge doors open and light floods the room.

"I know she was here, and I didn't see her leave," a

HYDRA guard mutters. "She was with that new Ranger guy all night."

"She's just a secretary, isn't she? What kind of trouble could she cause?" his partner asks.

"She's a computer operator, one of those hacker geniuses. What I heard was that she wanted to get in on the fighting, so she had the computer assign her to the tank corps. She and a sub-commander were the only ones to come back from a mission yesterday. They stuck her back in computers, but she's pretty suspicious if you ask me."

"Ah—you're just trying to make trouble for her 'cause she wouldn't dance with you."

You can tell the HYDRA guards are searching more thoroughly now, looking behind the bars and under tables. At any moment they will discover you. You hear the sound of a bolt being pulled back on a rifle, so you stand up and hurl your shield toward the noise.

Make an Agility with Shield FEAT by rolling one die and adding the result to your Agility with Shield ability. If the total is 17, turn to **200**. If it is 18 or 19, turn to **15**. If it is 20 or more, turn to **63**.

109 You move toward the warehouse to find a phone to alert the authorities. A peculiar humming starts behind you. Spinning around, you are just in time to witness the disappearance of your captives. One moment they are silhouetted by an eerie glow of light, and the next they are gone without a trace.

They must each have been wearing some sort of device so Viper could transport them away. If I had thought about it, I might have removed it, you chide yourself. Turn to **21**.

Your shield crashes into Viper's back, slam- **110** ming her across the control panel so that she lands across several buttons at once. The serpent's stare pattern disappears, but the list of rocket buyers remains.

Viper spins about with her laser pistol aimed at your middle, but you knock it from her grasp with a kick.

If you want to grapple with Viper for her teleporter ring, turn to **203**. If you think you should try to knock her out first, go to **66**.

As you stalk up on Viper, you are acutely **111** aware of every molecule on the floor that might betray you with a noise. Your eyes change focus continuously—from your feet to the door and back again as you tiptoe to where you can see her.

Clad in a green, skin-tight body suit, she leans casually against the desk. Behind you, a resounding THWACK indicates that Agent Hoffman has caught Blacklash unawares. Viper spins about, sees you, and raises her gun—a dangerous-looking energy weapon.

You hurl your shield at her. Make a Shield FEAT by rolling one die and adding the result to your Shield ability. If the total is 18 or less, move on to **33**. If it is 19, 20 or 21, proceed to **197**. If the total is 22 or more, turn to **79**.

As you roll away from the hostile mechanical **112** creature, several of its blades scrape along your shield. There is no damage, and you are unharmed.

Once you are out of the robot's sight, the mechanoid ignores you and begins homing in on Namor. *Not a moment too soon*, you think, since the Atlantean has just escaped the ring of fire in which he was trapped by smothering the flame with floor boards torn from the floor.

You notice that, though Namor could simply fly away from the robot, instead he grabs angrily at one of its legs and hurls the metal creature into a wall, scattering its components about the room. Turn to **178**.

113 You can't pass up this opportunity to capture Viper. Even if you miss her, which is a possibility, you can at least keep the HYDRA agents from harming any innocent bystanders.

You signal Agents Hoffman and Bronder to continue with the undercover mission, indicating by a nod that they are to follow the HYDRA commander's orders and get into the tanks.

Turn to **189**.

114 You charge into Nitro, but he's a lot stronger than you expect, and he does not fall away from the door. The two of you brawl in the doorway. Nitro kicks you with an exploding foot. You must subtract 6 from your Health points. Turn to **45**.

115 Viper aims a remarkable kick at your head, but you block it with one hand, knocking her off balance. She falls to the floor but rolls away from you expertly.

A second later, however, she shrieks! It is obvious from her expression that she is in great pain.

You see, then, protruding from her shoulder, the venom dart she'd meant for you.

You bend over her, removing the dart from her flesh. It was buried deep. "Hang on, Viper. SHIELD will have the anti-venom. We'll get it to you," you promise.

"Don't be disgusting," Viper spits at you. Before you are aware that she is still capable of movement, she manages to activate her teleporter ring. She glows and disappears.

Nick Fury runs into the information center. "Are you okay, Cap?" he asks upon seeing you kneeling on the ground.

"Just fine."

"I heard a scream. What happened to Viper?"

"I'm not sure." Quickly you explain to Fury how Viper fell on her own poisoned weaponry. "She didn't appear to be immune to the venom," you note.

"Maybe she had some anti-venom wherever she teleported to. I wonder if she'll have the strength to administer herself a dose."

You point to the list on the display screen. "Viper claimed those are all the people she sold rockets to."

"That's a terrific find!" Fury declares. "Hoffman and Bronder managed to sabotage Viper's cargo teleportation room and capture most of the missiles. With this list, we should just about be able to tie this case up."

You nod quietly. Despite all her evil intentions, it disturbs you to think that Viper might die with no one to aid her.

Sensing your concern, Fury tries to reassure you. "Cap, it wasn't your fault."

"I know. But now, of course, we'll have to wait to find out if she survived."

"Knowing Viper, if she is alive, she won't keep us guessing long," Fury assures.

"I guess not," you agree, wondering which is worse, not knowing Viper's fate, or finding out for sure.

Your adventure ends here. You are free to start again, but you must subtract 1 from your initial Karma total.

You pick yourself off the ground, warily eyeing the mist that indicates Nitro's vapor state. **116**

"Are you going to form back into a person so I can get a crack at you, Nitro?" you call out.

Apparently your attacker thinks that, having survived his first onslaught, you might be too tough for him. Nitro's mist form flees swiftly over the bay. Soon it is out of sight.

You cross the warehouse yard to check on Blacklash, who was also caught by the explosion. As you approach, the super villain warns you, "Keep back, Captain America!" and cracks his whip in your direction.

Before you can rush him, however, Blacklash begins to glow eerily, and a humming noise fills the air about him. He disappears, leaving only the rocket to prove he'd ever been there.

"He must have teleported back to Viper," you guess.

Turn to **21**.

117 You wait in front of Freedom Flight's headquarters as Agents Bronder and Hoffman dismiss the SHIELD cars that arrive as backup. A truck trailer pulls up—a secret SHIELD mobile office. You are ushered inside by none other than Nick Fury, director of SHIELD.

"Still determined to stay involved in this madness after last night and this morning?" Fury asks you as he locks the truck door.

"It doesn't make sense to quit while I'm behind," you reply with a grin. "If you have a plan to get Viper, I want to help. So tell me what it's all about?"

Turn to **198**.

118 Grabbing Agent Bronder's hand, you dash out of the lounge and across the corridor.

"The elevator won't take us anywhere without a passkey," Bronder whispers.

Another guard comes around the corner and spots you. "No one's supposed to be here past curfew—" he begins to say when he recognizes your red, white, and blue costume.

He raises his rifle, but Agent Bronder fires the one she is holding first, a warning shot at his feet, sending the guard scurrying back around the corner.

"Where does that lead?" you ask, pointing at the

only other exit available, a steel door at the end of the corridor.

"I only got to study the layout maps on the computer for a few minutes. Sorry, I don't remember that one," the woman apologizes.

"No time like the present for finding out," you comment.

You must smash the lock on the door with your shield. You are rewarded by the sight of a staircase leading up. A cool draft blows down on you. "It goes to the roof! Come on!"

One flight up, you come out onto a rooftop heliport. The building is only five stories high. "We can rappel down the side," you suggest, spotting a large coil of rope.

"Flying down would be easier," your companion counters, nodding to the two helicopters parked nearby.

"Can you fly one?" you ask.

Bronder nods.

"Excellent," you declare. "Go start one up."

You tie the handle of the door to the roof down to a pole by the stair shaft. It won't hold long, but it's better than nothing. You run up to the helicopter Agent Bronder has started, but she is climbing down from it.

"What's wrong?" you shout over the noise.

"The engine's bad," she answers. "Can't you hear it?"

"I'll take your word for it."

The two of you run for the other copter. Glancing back you see the door being pushed against the rope. You watch the SHIELD agent hotwire the second helicopter. Just as you see her give the 'go' sign with her upturned thumb, and you circle around to the passenger side, you hear, over the roar of the helicopter, the sound of the roof door being smashed open.

Rifle fire pelts the blacktop on the roof, making a line toward you. Make an Agility FEAT by rolling one die and adding the result to your Agility ability. If the total is 11 or less, turn to **179**. If it is 12 or better, turn to **206**.

119 The Wasp guides you to the medical facilities and with a gentle hand washes your wound and sprays it with a clear fluid that makes it feel better almost immediately.

"What is that stuff?" you ask.

"Something to make you heal faster."

"Chicken soup?"

"Very funny. It's something new we're testing out for research. How do you feel?"

"Like a new man," you assure her. And indeed you do. Add 3 points to your Health point total.

"Yeah, well, take it easy anyway," your fellow Avenger warns, slapping a large bandage on your cut and a clear adhesive patch over the hole in your costume.

"Yes, ma'am," you promise.

Bidding Jan good afternoon, you take the elevator to

104

the main floor of the mansion and head out to the street.

Turn to **172**.

As you begin climbing the steps, an uneasy **120** feeling comes over you. "Do you notice anything strange?" you whisper.

Bronder and Hoffman both shake their heads.

Shrugging your shoulders, you begin taking the steps more quickly, until you find that the sixteenth step goes down—a long way—at least fifteen feet. You must subtract 3 points from your Health because the fall knocks the wind out of you and leaves you with several bruises.

Your flashlight reveals a perfectly round pit with laser-polished walls. Above you is the bottom of the staircase. Agent Bronder's head comes popping through it. "Are you all right?" she whispers.

"Fine, just bruises on my body and ego," you reply.

"The rest of the stairs are holographic projections," Agent Hoffman says as his head, too, appears through the mirage.

"Yes, to disguise this trap," you reply.

"Gee, there aren't any snakes down there," Agent Bronder scoffs, dropping the end of a rope down to you. "What kind of self-respecting pit doesn't have snakes in it?"

"Or pointy stakes at least," Agent Hoffman adds as he helps tug on the rope you are climbing.

"I assure you," you say, reaching the top, "that if Viper knew we were coming, she would have arranged something special. Let's go."

Turn to **154**.

Taking a deep breath to clear your head, you **121** instantly take stock of the situation. Agent Bronder, having survived Nitro's blast by ducking under the loading dock, is now quite efficiently preparing to scoop Nitro's gaseous form into her Nitro-buster. She is unaware that Blacklash is about to lay her out with a blow from his steel whip!

Must stop him, you resolve, throwing your shield. Make a Shield FEAT by rolling one die and adding the result to your Shield ability. If the total is 18 or less, turn to **150**. If it is 19 or more, turn to **3**.

122 You manage to remain standing, and with a supreme effort, you detach the bola and toss it at Blacklash before he can pull out his whip again. The bola wraps about the villain's arm.

Dropping his whip and grabbing for the bola with his opposite hand, Blacklash cries, "Aargh! I think I've dislocated my shoulder! Get him!" he orders Nitro.

Turn to **4**.

123 "I wonder how Laura's doing," the SHIELD agent mutters.

"Just fine and dandy, thank you," a familiar voice answers from the hallway door. Agent Bronder stands there, without her mask.

You and Hoffman follow her lead and remove the HYDRA masks. You take off the shirt to the Turtle costume, as well, and retrieve your shield.

"Did you do that?" Hoffman asks his partner, pointing to the hole in the wall caused by the tank.

"I had to," says Agent Bronder. "I was under orders from the commander. Glad to see you cleaned his clock. So where's Viper?"

"I don't think she was ever here or going to be," you reply.

"The HYDRA commander said they overheard a conversation between Viper and Mr. Gress."

"But I'm Mr. Gress, and I don't know anyone by the name of Viper," protests the man HYDRA Commander Wright was interrogating.

"Isn't there another Mr. Gress, sir?" you ask.

"Why, yes. My cousin, Aaron. I'm Kurt Gress. But Aaron's still in New York, finishing some business."

"At the Staten Island headquarters, making a deal with Viper," Agent Hoffman guesses.

"It seems likely," you reply.

"If you civilians would step outside, please," Agent Bronder says, "Administrator Johnson of SHIELD will debrief you all."

"What's SHIELD," one of the former prisoners asks, and who are you?"

"Please, it will all be explained outside," Bronder says, ushering the group out.

"How did SHIELD get here so fast?" you ask.

"I radioed them from the tank as soon as I got in it," she replies.

"But you were in there with four other HYDRA agents," Agent Hoffman says.

"I just flipped the transceiver switch and adjusted the frequency to SHIELD's while people were busy getting settled, and then I tapped the message out in Morse code on the microphone. They thought I was just nervous. The quality of HYDRA agents is really slipping."

"Yeah, especially their tank drivers," Hoffman mutters.

If you already know the location of Viper's secret base, turn to **12**. If you haven't gotten this information yet, go to **49**.

A visit to a Veteran's Administration hospital **124** confirms that your battle left you stiff, sore, and bruised, but with no broken bones.

"You took quite a beating there," the doctor on call notes.

"I know you super hero types probably think you'll live forever, but not at the rate you're going you won't. You're lucky it wasn't worse."

"I know," you reply.

"Well, since you don't want me to prescribe anything for pain, all I can recommend is rest. At least two days. Take it or leave it."

As you get back into your van, you wonder, *Should I be a good boy and take it easy today like the doctor said? Or should I go out checking for more clues as to what Viper is up to before the trail gets cold?*

If you are going to rest today and do nothing more taxing than thinking, go to **164**. If you feel you can't afford to take the day off and want to continue your investigation right away, turn to **177**.

125 Your shield shears through the robot's ankle and rolls to a stop against the mosquito netting the Wasp tossed aside. The robot teeters on one leg for a few seconds before it crashes to the floor. It's still trying to lash out with its weaponry, but it's no longer able to follow you.

Add 1 to your Karma total.

The way ahead of you seems clear. You can try to sprint across the room without your shield while the coast is clear (**145**), but you might be safer taking the time to retrieve it (**18**).

126 With a tremendous thrust, you roll backward, reversing Viper's hold and trapping her beneath you. You are careful to avoid her mouth. Turn to **203**.

127 In the next room, Agent Bronder cries out in pain. Grabbing up your shield, you dash back into the cellar. As you suspected would be the case, battling inside has severely limited Blacklash's ability to utilize his whips. Yet the villain has other weapons. He has

108

already pinned Agent Bronder under his gravity bolo which generates an artificial force nearly impossible to fight. Now he is trying to entangle Agent Hoffman in his necro-lash.

You must stop Blacklash before he sends a deadly jolt of electricity through the necro-lash. You lunge at your foe. To grab him, make a Strength FEAT by rolling one die and adding the result to your Strength. If the total is 7 or less, turn to **23**. If it is 8 or more, go to **104**.

Your blow lands on the HYDRA agent's chin, **128** but his rifle still goes off in your direction. You must subtract 2 from your Health points, as the bullet grazes your arm.

Turn to **37**.

Trusting Constrictor's information, you con- **129** sider seriously the danger involved. *Viper usually has quite a few resources at hand, not to mention henchmen. I'd better call in some reserves of my own.*

You do not alert the Avengers, however, but a group that has a stronger interest in Viper and her schemes—SHIELD. This morning you had already made plans to call the intelligence agency, but now you'll be giving them information, not asking for it.

Your phone call is put through immediately to Nick Fury, the director of SHIELD, a long-time friend and associate, but he sounds rushed.

"Don't have time to chat, Cap," the gruff colonel informs you. "Is it important?"

"Could be, Nick," you answer. "I got a tip that the Viper would be up to something tonight."

"The Viper!" Fury's tone is suddenly more excited. "Well, in that case, where have you been? I've been waiting for your call all day," he jokes. "What did you hear?"

"Well, the source is questionable—I got the tip from Constrictor—but I believe him."

"He's certainly not on friendly terms with the witch," Fury agrees. "What did he say?"

"That if I was at the Curtis Supply Warehouse tonight at midnight I might see something of interest—something about the rocket's red glare."

"Oh, boy," Fury breathes. "When you stumble onto something, you do it in a big way."

"Then you think Constrictor was on the level?" you ask.

"We can't talk about this over the phone. I'll send some agents—Hoffman and Bronder—out to meet you there at twenty-two hundred hours. They'll be in jogging suits. I'll make sure they know you're the boss and to keep their backup out of your way."

"All right, Nick," you agree.

It must be something big, you think, *for Fury to be so secretive about it.*

Turn to **134**.

130 The super villain's whip lands across Agent Bronder's back with a sickening tearing sound. She falls to the ground, her Nitro-buster clattering noisily onto the concrete.

Nitro's glittering cloud form does not coalesce back into human shape, though. Instead it flees—drifting swiftly out over the bay.

Must have been scared off by Agent Bronder's vacuum device, you guess.

Blacklash, faced with his partner's desertion, and seeing Agent Hoffman appear beside you, snarls and retracts his whips. You think he is about to surrender, when a glowing silhouette surrounds him and he disappears.

You and Hoffman run to Agent Bronder's side. She is still conscious, but dazed looking. There is a huge tear up the back of her sweatshirt, revealing a gray plastic material underneath.

"Was that a moose or a grizzly?" the female SHIELD agent moans.

"Blacklash's whip," you answer. "You're lucky to be breathing."

"Protective vest," the woman gasps. "Should have worn plate mail, though."

"At least we got the rocket," Agent Hoffman sighs.

You nod. Add 2 to your Karma points for helping to stop Viper's henchmen from launching it.

"Great," Bronder growls. "With the eighteen Intelligence has accounted for, that makes nineteen out of six hundred."

"Six hundred!" you gasp.

"That's right. Six hundred. Viper hijacked them from Uncle Sam," Hoffman tells you.

Peering at the rocket, you can just make out a U.S. Government stamp on the missile's steel casing.

"Told you all the action would be bay side," Bronder nudges her partner.

"Not necessarily. I caught the owner of this place, Steven Curtis, sneaking around the trucks. Claims he refused to buy a rocket from Viper, so she's trying to frame him."

"It's possible," Bronder nods. "Viper has been strictly cash-and-carry with this operation. If she was selling this rocket, she'd have been here to take the money. Not the sort of thing she would entrust to her flunkies."

"And if she made it look as if this Mr. Curtis launched the rocket," you point out, "it would be easier to convince his enemies to buy one. Who did Curtis think Viper would want to strike?" you ask.

"Probably Freedom Flight," Hoffman explains. "That's an anti-Doom group with its headquarters just south across the bay, on Staten Island. Curtis is a founding member of the PCL—People's Choice of Latveria. They practically worship Victor Von Doom, though he couldn't tell them from ants on the ground."

"Why?" you ask, astonished that anyone would support the would-be world conqueror. You have fought against the ruler of Latveria yourself, and in your opinion, he is not sane.

111

"He may be a pain in the tail for the rest of the world," Bronder sighs, "but he's the best leader Latveria's had since 1512."

"Doom is just a back-alley issue here," says Hoffman. "It's what Viper is trying to do to the whole country with these rockets that we've got to stop."

"She's trying to incite violence between each and every different political faction in the country," you add. "Then, in the chaos, she'll try to destroy the government or make a play for power herself."

"Precisely. And with Blacklash analyzing the rockets' electronic components for her, she could start making her own. We could be chasing her until doomsday—literally."

"So what do you suggest our next step be?" you ask.

"Well, before you showed up with your tip, we had a tip of our own we were going to start following. It will require some undercover work. Care to join us?"

You nod. "How could I turn you down?"

Turn to **13**.

131 As you begin climbing the steps, you start to feel uneasy. *What am I being so silly about?* you wonder, and you proceed up the steps faster. Suddenly, you plunge through a step as though it is made of air and slip down a slick cliff wall! You land at least fifteen feet, twisting your ankle as you hit the bottom. You must subtract 3 from your Health points.

Your flashlight reveals a round pit with laser-polished walls. Looking up you can see you the bottom of the staircase you were climbing. Turning off your flashlight you still see it—it glows eerily on its own.

*It's a holographic projection of steps, your realize.
And it covers this trap. Viper's doing, no doubt. I must
be close to her lair.*

If you have no Health points left, you are in no shape
to continue this adventure. If you have between 1 and
10 Health points, you must make an Endurance FEAT
by rolling one die and adding the result to your Endurance ability. If the total is 10 or less, turn to **95**. If the
total is 11 or more, or if you have 10 or more Health
points, turn to **35**.

"I'm sorry, Jan," you say, declining the invi- **132**
tation. "Another day perhaps."

The Wasp gives a little sigh. "Okay. Excuse me, then.
I have to see if I can scare up Dane," she says, referring
to the Avenger known as the Black Knight. "I need the
exercise even if you don't!"

As you step out the door, you feel bad about refusing
the Wasp's request. The practice might have been good
for you. Subtract 1 Karma point from your total.

You decide you are too keyed up to cycle around the
city on your Harley-Davidson, so you head down Fifth
Avenue on foot. Turn to **214**.

When you and Agent Bronder reach SHIELD **133**
headquarters, Nick Fury and Bronder's partner, Ken
Hoffman, are already waiting.

"Where?" is the first question Fury has for the two of
you.

"Pittsburgh, Pennsylvania," Agent Bronder answers
immediately. "Under something called the Incline, we
were told."

"That's one of those hillside cable cars, isn't it?"
Fury asks you.

You nod, recalling a battle you fought alongside the
Avengers at that exact same location. "Viper has probably tunneled warrens all through the mountains."

"We can't thank you enough for bringing this stray

sheep home," Fury says, jerking his head in Bronder's direction.

"My pleasure," you reply, smiling at Agent Bronder, who looks rebellious at the thought of needing to be rescued.

Add 5 points to your Karma for rescuing Agent Bronder and getting the information she had to SHIELD.

"So, do you want to get in on this?" Fury asks. "You've earned it."

"Yes, please," you answer. "Catching the Viper would be more than enough reward."

Turn to **186**.

134 At dusk you drive down to Newark in your customized van and park opposite the object of your stakeout. The Curtis Supply Warehouse is a clean, new building, and the warehouse yard, which borders on Newark Bay, is well lit, but the only other security about the building is a high chain-link fence. To avoid being spotted, you observe the scenery from your van's periscope.

Motor traffic is very light, and no pedestrians pass you until just before ten o'clock, when a man and a woman jog by dressed in warm-up suits. *Must be Nick's agents*, you guess as they turn the corner. *I'd better be ready to greet them on their next pass.*

You slip quickly out of the van. Waiting in an alleyway, you listen for the sound of rubber pounding the pavement. After the joggers pass you again, you join them, running at their pace.

"I thought you said this neighborhood was safe," the woman jokes to her partner in a panting voice, obviously meant to be overheard.

"Hoffman and Bronder, I presume," you reply.

"I'm Bronder. He's Hoffman," the woman answers.

"You must be Captain America," Hoffman says.

"Well, he isn't Spider-Man," Bronder snaps as the three of you turn the corner. "Can we stop running now?"

"I know he's not," Hoffman retorts as the three of you slow to a walk. "Spider-Man doesn't carry a shield."

"He has to show off everything he learned in his advanced training course—SHIELD VIPs 101," Bronder tells you.

"Is that a prerequisite for field work?" you ask.

"No. For field work all you need is a field. That's our car," Bronder adds, pointing up the street. "We have to get some equipment out of it."

"We've been trying to get a line on Viper since last month. She's been selling rockets," Hoffman explains. "We caught someone trying to smuggle one back home to Ireland, and someone else shipping his to South America, but most of them seemed to have been purchased for domestic use."

"So Constrictor wasn't just using a figure of speech when he said I'd see something by the rocket's red glare," you comment.

"Unfortunately, no. Someone in Florida took out a Communist Party headquarters with their rocket. One in Chicago hit an Arab social center. We found one in an LA street gang hangout. We've managed to keep it under wraps that these incidents were related—so far—but if it gets out that these things are available to the home market, we'll have panic."

"Viper's schemes were always insidious," you remark while the agents strap equipment belts around their waists.

"Tell him about the grandmother—that's my favorite," Bronder quips, handing you a SHIELD walkie-talkie.

"Some kid reported his grandmother had one in her condominium. She's a Daughter of the American Revolution. Doesn't want the Japanese to open a car plant in her neighborhood."

"What's that for?" you ask as Agent Bronder draws out what looks like a cross between two scuba air tanks and a vacuum cleaner.

"That's our Nitro-buster," Agent Bronder answers. "You see, we know Blacklash is working for Viper—you know him?"

"Yes, we've fought before," you reply, remembering Blacklash's painfully effective specialty, cybernetically controlled whips.

"Well, last week, Blacklash helped break Nitro, the exploding man, out of a prison infirmary. We suspect he was acting on Viper's instructions. She's going to be needing more muscle to expand her operation. Anyway, this little device," Bronder explains, holding up the Nitro-buster, "will contain Nitro once he blows up. Some of his gaseous form will be sucked into one tank and the rest of him into the other."

"So he can't reintegrate," you say, nodding in understanding. Nitro, as you know, can reintegrate and blow up an apparently unlimited number of times, but if he can't re-form, he can't blow up. "But you'll have to get him to blow up first," you point out. "Won't that be dangerous?"

"Hah! Danger is my name," Agent Bronder says, tossing her hair back.

"No, it's not," Agent Hoffman corrects in a joke he's probably made before. "It's Laura."

Agent Bronder makes a face at her partner.

"Colonel Fury said to show you this," Agent Hoffman says, handing you a sheet of paper. "It's a search warrant for the warehouse. He said you were very picky about this sort of thing."

"Everything appears to be in order," you comment after examining the warrant. "Shall we begin?"

The three of you jog back toward the warehouse. Moving as one, you climb the chain-link fence and

sneak across the warehouse yard. Hidden in the shadows, you discuss your strategy.

"Viper has a teleporter," you remember out loud.

"Yes, we know," Hoffman nods. "She could come in anywhere with it. We'll have to split up to keep watch. Someone on the bay side of the warehouse, someone inside, and the third one of us here watching the truck yard."

"They'll never do business in the truck yard," Agent Bronder argues. "It's too open."

"They could teleport right inside one of those big old truck trailers. Then whoever's buying the rocket would only have to hook a cab up to it and drive it someplace safe," Hoffman answers.

"What place could be safer than inside the warehouse, or just launching it from the dock tonight?" his partner argues.

"Look, I'll take the truck yard," Hoffman says. "What do you want?"

"I can't decide," Bronder sighs. "You pick next, Captain," she offers.

If you want to stake out the inside of the warehouse, turn to **19**. If you'd rather watch the bay side of the warehouse yard, go to **157**.

117

135 Your shield smacks into Blacklash's shoulder. He pulls back from the rocket control panel with a scream of pain. Before he can recover, you run forward to retrieve your shield.

Blacklash is no longer your most pressing problem. Checking on the cry of his partner, Nitro comes running from the building.

Make a Reason FEAT by rolling one die and adding the result to your Reason ability. If the total is 5 or less, turn to **148**. If it is 6 or more, turn to **4**.

136 The spirit of freedom you have fought for all your life fills you with the will to move. You jerk your head around so your gaze is torn from the screen. The effect of the serpent stare takes a moment to fade. Carefully keeping your eyes on Viper, you aim your shield at her.

Make a Shield FEAT by rolling one die and adding the result to your Shield ability. If the total is 18 or less, turn to **71**. If it is 19 or more, turn to **110**.

137 You get a secure grip on the rifle and use it to push the HYDRA leader back against the wall.

Your foe gasps as you shove the rifle tight against him, pinning him down. He growls at you like some sort of wild animal.

You push harder. "Are you going to behave?" you demand.

If you have less than 10 Health points, turn to **29**. If you have 10 or more Health points, proceed to **194**.

Your speed simply isn't fast enough, and one **138** of the robot's machetes slashes at your calf, cutting through your boot, your body suit, and the upper layers of your skin. Subtract 5 points from your Health point total. You may not subtract any of this damage from your Karma.

Fortunately, before the robot is able to slice at you again, Captain Marvel fires an energy bolt at it. With a quick sizzle, the robot's power dies. Your attacker topples with a crash and is still.

"You okay?" your partner calls.

"Nothing wrong worth writing home about," you answer, sounding cheerier than you feel so C.M. won't be concerned. Your wound from the robot isn't bleeding much, but it sure does smart.

Turn to **175**.

You catch the guard in a tight headlock. **139** Stunned by the force of your hold, the guard drops his weapon—a nasty looking stun gun. Agent Hoffman slides the van door open and hops out.

"Bronder, get out!" you order the other SHIELD agent, who is still sparring with the remaining HYDRA recruit. Not until she dives out the door do you climb out with your prisoner.

Turn to **32**.

After grabbing a few hours sleep, you meet **140** Agents Hoffman and Bronder early the next morning in front of Freedom Flight's Staten Island headquarters, a modest two-story office building surrounded by a small yard.

"They've gone," Agent Hoffman tells you when you pull up on your motorcycle.

"Gone where?" you ask.

"To a new headquarters in Philadelphia," Hoffman answers. "So the rocket last night wouldn't have hurt anyone even if it had been launched."

"No, that makes sense," you say. "Viper's not dumb—she wouldn't be able to sell another rocket if they were all dead."

"You think she warned them?" Bronder asks.

"Maybe," you reply, feeling confused. "But maybe their moving was just a coincidence—Viper wants to promote death—encouraging revenge will help her sell her bombs."

"So, if they're buying a rocket from Viper, will they meet her here or at their new place in Philly?" Hoffman asks.

"Nitro said their meeting was supposed to take place in a secret passage. Someone could be hiding inside right now."

"But Viper couldn't have planned to meet anyone here if she was going to bomb the building," Bronder argues, sounding exasperated.

"Is the building locked?" you ask.

"We got the key from the owner," Agent Hoffman answers.

"If you were going to be bombed, where would you hide?"

"In another city, like Philadelphia," Bronder quips.

"The basement!" Agent Hoffman answers.

The three of you investigate the basement of the building. Examining the walls carefully, you come to a section that doesn't quite meet the floor. Finding a loose brick, you push. A section of the wall swings back revealing a room containing a desk, a chair, a cot, and a phone. There is a door in the back of the room.

"This is it," Hoffman whistles—when suddenly the phone rings.

Without hesitating, you answer it. "Hello," you say, trying to disguise your voice.

120

"Good morning, Mr. Gress," a woman's voice replies. You recognize it immediately. It's Viper!

"I'm sorry to inform you," the sultry voice continues, "that the authorities caught Mr. Curtis last night before he was able to launch his rocket and destroy your headquarters."

"I already noticed that the building was still here," you answer wryly.

On the other end, the Viper laughs gaily. "Very amusing, but I'm afraid this means you're on your own trying to convince your fellow Freedom Flighters to spend their money on one of my rockets."

"No. I have the money," you tell her.

"Really? What did you do, rob a bank?"

"Maybe."

Viper laughs. "Well, then, I see no reason to put this off until tomorrow. I'll be there in ten minutes."

"I need more time," you argue.

"Look, I haven't time for games. If you want the rocket, be there, alone, with the five grand."

Turn to **190**.

Your shield strikes the wall behind Blacklash **141** and rebounds toward the villain. But the injury to your hand as you pulled it out of the metal strap has affected your aim, and the shield does not hit the villain squarely enough to put him off balance.

"Now you're going to get it," Blacklash snarls. Snatching up a hypodermic from a table he injects you with its unknown contents. Within moments the walls spin about you, then all is black.

You pass what seems like days in uneasy sleep and horrible nightmares. Then finally you wake to a relatively cheerful sight—the face of your friend, Nick Fury, the director of SHIELD.

"I was afraid I'd never see those baby blues open again," the former Army Colonel says, smiling. "How are you, Cap?"

"Confused, a little groggy still. What happened?" You find yourself smiling with relief.

"Well, to cut a long story short, we were following HYDRA to Viper's secret base. HYDRA was attacking Viper to get some rockets they claim she stole from them. Actually, she stole them from Uncle Sam, which is what HYDRA had planned to do."

Your head swims with the thought that HYDRA, an international crime syndicate as bent on world domination as Viper is, is also messed up in this affair. "I was trying to stop Blacklash and Nitro from launching one of those rockets when I was captured," you explain.

Fury ignores your crestfallen tones. "Right. Viper stole six hundred of those babies. But HYDRA stormed her headquarters with the help of Nitro, who was apparently dissatisfied with his lot under Viper's command. Viper and Blacklash fled. HYDRA ran off with the rockets, and we found the abandoned base and you inside. Viper must have left you for dead. You had enough viper venom in you to kill an elephant. First medic who looked at you thought you were dead, but I wouldn't take his word for it. I know what a heavy sleeper you are," Fury jokes.

"What will you do to get the rockets back from HYDRA? And do you have any leads on Viper?"

"We've got some people on HYDRA. We expect HYDRA will try to unload the rockets overseas. Viper was trying to cause trouble with them here at home. As for her whereabouts, who knows. With that teleporter ring, she could be anywhere. Do me a favor, Cap?"

"Sure, Nick."

"Take it easy. Rest and get better. You can tackle Viper another day."

"I'll do that," you agree. "Both those things."

Your adventure ends here. You may begin again, subtracting 1 from your initial Health total and 2 from your Karma for what you lost and what you learned.

You tackle Blacklash and knock him to the **142** ground.

Blacklash screams, "My arm! You broke my arm!"

Well, that's one less whip he can crack at me, you think. *Now to neutralize Nitro.*

Make a Reason FEAT by rolling one die and adding the result to your Reason ability. If the total is 5 or less, go to **148**. If it is 6 or more, proceed to **40.**

You get some sleep during what's left of the **143** night, which leaves you feeling a little better. Add 2 points to your Health.

Then you ride your cycle to the rendezvous point you agreed upon with SHIELD. Agent Hoffman, the young man who caught Mr. Curtis the evening before, ushers you into a SHIELD mobile office in an unmarked truck trailer. Nick Fury is already within. Seated next to him is a young woman.

"Welcome, Cap," Fury greets you. He points to the young man, saying, "Ken Hoffman you met last night. And this is his partner," he says, nodding toward the young woman, "Laura Bronder. Thought you'd like to know we picked up Nitro this morning. He wasn't real happy working for Viper. He slipped his leash this morning after she teleported him to Atlantic City, and he somehow wandered into our net."

"Has he given you any information?" you ask.

Fury shakes his head. "Not much. He claims Viper wouldn't tell him anything and that he didn't even know the location of her base—that he only went in and out of it via the teleporter. I have some other agents chasing the only lead he could give us, but I doubt it will pan out. Anyway, to the business at hand. Agents Bronder and Hoffman have both been working on the Viper case since last month when the snaky lady stole those rockets she's been selling from Uncle Sam."

"How many rockets?" you ask. You expect him to say three or four.

"Six hundred," Agent Bronder answers. "And we think she's got Blacklash trying to copy them for her."

You whistle in surprise. "So how do we catch Viper and recover the rockets?"

Turn to **198**.

144 Weakened by the blast you took from Viper's weapon, you are unable to shake her grip quickly enough to avoid her attack. Like a snake, she darts her head down to your arm, and she pierces your costume and your skin with her teeth. You must subtract 10 from your Health points.

Your arm stings, burns, and goes numb in the space of a few seconds. You raise your opposite arm to deliver a blow before the poison can affect your whole body, but Viper has moved away quickly. Through blurring vision, you watch her glow and disappear.

You note that the giant screen no longer displays the serpent stare pattern, but the list of rocket buyers remains. It is hard to feel very satisfied over this victory, though, as you collapse, gasping for air.

You cannot see, but you can hear Nick Fury shouting orders.

His voice sounds as though it's a long way off, but you realize groggily he must be right next to you, when you feel him shaking you as he calls your name, deep concern in his voice.

"She's poisoned him! Get the medics! Make sure they bring that anti-venom formula. Hurry!" Fury barks. "Hang in there, Cap. Help's on the way."

You know you'll pull through this with SHIELD's help and recover from the pain, but it will be much longer before you recover from the frustration of losing Viper again.

Your adventure ends here. You may begin again, subtracting 1 from your initial Health and 1 from your initial Karma.

You sprint across the room before the com- **145**
puter launches another mechanism after you. Then you look down into the basket that holds your team's goal. It turns out to be a Ping-Pong-sized ball surrounded by an eery red light.

If you want to wait for your partner to reach for the ball, turn to **202**. If you want to try to fish out the ball with your hands, turn to **8**.

You grab the rifle with both hands and give it **146**
a sharp twist up, sending the muzzle of the weapon cracking against your foe's face. The expression on his face goes blank and he slides to the floor.

Turn to **184**.

Summoned via walkie-talkie by Agent Bron- **147**
der, SHIELD's backup pulls up in two SHIELD cars accompanied by a truck trailer that is to serve as a base

of operations. The backup teams take over guarding the prisoners and start to move the rocket back into the safety of government hands. In the meantime, Agent Hoffman informs you that it wasn't all that dull in back of the warehouse, either.

"I caught the owner of the place, Steven Curtis, sneaking around. He claims Viper is trying to frame him."

"Do you think he might have been here to buy the rocket?" you ask.

"Not really. He hasn't got any money on him. But maybe Blacklash can tell us otherwise."

"Look," Agent Bronder says, nodding her head in the direction of the gate. "It's Colonel Fury."

Nick Fury, dressed in a tux, alights from a limousine and walks toward you. He has an eager, satisfied look on his face.

"I just got the news," Fury says. "Congratulations, you three! I hear you took prisoners. Have they been interrogated yet?"

PROPERTY OF U.S. GOVERNMENT

"Um, Nitro is in no condition to talk," Hoffman explains, "but Blacklash has been disarmed and is wide awake and, we hope, ready to talk. We were just going in to speak with him."

"Carry on," Fury orders. "I'll be in in a few minutes with Cap."

Hoffman and Bronder salute and head for the truck trailer that serves as a mobile SHIELD base of operations.

Fury lights a cigar as he watches the flurry around him—some agents lowering the rocket onto a dolly, others moving Nitro into an ambulance, and others interviewing an elderly man who you guess must be Hoffman's prisoner, Mr. Curtis.

"I hope we didn't spoil your evening, Nick," you say, pointing to Fury's formal evening attire.

"Spoil it? You've just made it! You give me the perfect excuse to get out of some stupid political dinner, and you practically serve me Viper on a platter. I can't thank you enough."

Add 5 points to your Karma for helping SHIELD in this matter.

"We haven't got Viper yet," you point out.

"No, but Blacklash is the perfect appetizer. What did you think of Hoffman and Bronder?"

"They are very efficient," you reply.

"But a little unusual?"

"Yes," you admit.

"Hoffman is as methodical as a CPA, and Bronder is as tenacious as a bulldog. They're the perfect team. If I only had ten more of them and two more of you . . . ah, what I could do!"

You smile at the compliment. "I'd like to hear what Blacklash has to say," you tell Fury.

"By all means." The colonel waves you toward the SHIELD mobile office.

Inside, Blacklash has been stripped of his costume and now wears only khaki overalls. Though the criminal is relatively harmless now, two SHIELD agents stand guard on either side of the table at which he sits.

Agents Bronder and Hoffman are seated across from him. As you enter, they rise to give you and Fury their chairs.

"Hoffman and Bronder have been coordinating the hunt for Viper ever since she got hold of this rocket and five hundred and ninety-nine others just like it," Fury explains as he sits down.

"Six hundred!" you gasp in astonishment. "How do you know the number?"

"That's how many were hijacked from Uncle Sam last month," Fury answers.

Turn to **201**.

148 Nitro charges toward you, his eyes glowing. The next moment, you feel yourself caught up in the shock wave as Nitro explodes his whole body! You are slammed across the warehouse yard. Only the fence around the perimeter of the yard keeps you from splashing into the bay.

Subtract 15 Health points from your total. If your Health is 0 or less, your adventure ends here.

If you are still capable of action, make an Endurance FEAT roll by rolling one die and adding the result to your Endurance ability. If the total is 8 or less, turn to **162**. If it is 9 or more, turn to **116**.

149 You leap across the chasm with your arms outstretched to grab hold of the opposite edge. But you miss! By only a few inches, but you plunge downward into the darkness!

Fortunately, there are ledges on the way down that help slow your rate of descent as you catch onto them and they break off in your hands. When you finally stop you feel reasonably certain you haven't fallen more than fifty feet, but you can't tell because you've dropped your flashlight and everything around you is pitch black.

You've twisted your ankle badly, and you have an uncomfortable feeling that you have landed on another ledge and that the shaft goes down much deeper. You wait in the darkness rather than risk falling farther.

Turn to **168**.

The shock of the explosion must have put **150** you more off balance than you thought. Your shield misses Blacklash by several inches and disappears into the darkness. Turn to **130**.

"I'm sure you'll find something soon," you **151** murmur encouragingly to the SHIELD agent.

"I suppose," she sighs. "Well, I'm turning in. Say good night to Ken for me."

The next morning after an early breakfast and more exhausting fighting drills, you, Agent Hoffman, and four other men are separated from the rest. In deference to your skill, you are allowed to remain in your Turtle costume. The others are given official HYDRA uniforms complete with masks.

You are taken to the windowless minibus in the underground garage. Standing near the minibus, dressed in a HYDRA uniform, is Agent Bronder. She is holding her mask in one hand. As soon as she is sure you and Hoffman have seen her, she puts the mask on. You, Bronder, and Hoffman board the vehicle first, squeezing into the back seat together.

"Well?" Hoffman whispers to his partner eagerly.

"I had the computer assign me to a tank crew for this assault you're going on."

"Why? You're supposed to be assaulting the computer."

"The only thing I could get on Viper was the name of the HYDRA commander in charge of her capture. It's Bill Wright, and he's in charge of this mission. He's in Philadelphia, waiting for this unit. We're attacking Freedom Flight's Philadelphia headquarters. For some reason, HYDRA is sure Viper will be there this morning selling them a rocket."

"Good enough," you say, and you settle back for the journey to Philadelphia.

After more than an hour's drive, the bus finally stops, and you and the others debark inside another abandoned warehouse. The two veteran HYDRA agents who escorted you on the bus line you up for inspection by their commander, who stands waiting imperiously in front of two monstrous tanks!

After you accept the rifles handed to you, the HYDRA commander explains your mission. "To satisfy your curiosity, I can tell you that I am Commander Bill Wright, and we are in Philadelphia. We are going to attack the headquarters of a political group called Freedom Flight. We couldn't care less about Freedom Flight itself, but they are meeting this morning with a woman who calls herself Viper."

One of the veteran HYDRA agents unrolls a life-size poster of the Viper.

The commander continues. "She is to be captured alive, though not necessarily unharmed. Nothing else matters."

Where did HYDRA get this information, and how accurate is it . . . you wonder, *especially given that Viper and Blacklash still have the teleporter at their disposal?* Is it possible HYDRA will succeed where you could not?

You study the commander. *If he's in charge of capturing the Viper, as Agent Bronder said, he must know the location of Viper's secret base. Perhaps it would be easier to capture him and then tackle Viper's base with SHIELD,* you think.

If you believe you should go along with the HYDRA mission and try to capture Viper, turn to **113**. If you

130

would rather try to kidnap the HYDRA commander and make him tell you where Viper's hideout is, turn to **181**.

This is silly, you think. *I'm getting jumpy* **152** *over nothing. I shouldn't let my own impatience interfere with my obligations to my fellow Avengers.*

"That sounds like a good idea, Wasp. You're on," you say.

Down in the combat simulation room, Namor—AKA Sub-Mariner, former prince of Atlantis—and Captain Marvel are already waiting. Like you, Namor fought against the Axis Powers in World War II. He still appears young, due to his Atlantean blood, and he stands haughtily in the center of the room, apparently quite certain that the exercise to come will be child's play.

Captain Marvel, who has the amazing ability to transform herself into all known forms of electromagnetic energy, is limbering up quietly in the corner. Despite the fact that she is a full-fledged member of the Avengers, Captain Marvel still seems a little awed by all her super hero teammates.

"I thought you two captains might challenge Namor and I," the Wasp jokes. "If that's all right with you, that is."

You nod in agreement as Captain Marvel comes to stand by your side.

"Why don't you explain the rules to these two, Cap?" Jan asks.

"It's really quite simple," you say. "All four of us start at this end of the room. At the other end"—you point across the seemingly empty expanse of the gymnasium-sized room—"will be two baskets, each containing a ball. We have to go get them and carry them to the other side."

"Child's play," Namor scoffs, confirming your feeling that he is overconfident.

"Well, there are a few itty-bitty problems," Jan explains. "The room is full of hidden, computer-controlled defense mechanisms that will make it difficult to get across in either direction. The computer also sets up traps around the ball or within the ball itself that will prevent one member of each partnership from picking up or carrying the ball. The computer can change these defenses at random, so the opposite teammate may have to carry the ball instead. Also, you and I, Namor, can try to prevent Captain America and Captain Marvel from reaching their goal and vice versa."

Taking up where Jan left off, you detail the test further. "You lose points for the destruction of equipment or for seriously injuring another player. The computer defense mechanisms are as real as those of any opponent, so you can get hurt if you're not careful. The computer won't play friendly, but it will stop the game, if you're hurt badly."

"How nice," Captain Marvel says, grinning. "A chivalrous computer."

"Finally," you conclude, "we have five minutes to finish. If we finish early, we get points for all the seconds left on the clock, and bonus points for being the first team to finish. Oh, and you aren't allowed to leave the room," you warn Captain Marvel specifically, knowing she could pass through the walls and try to take the ball from the opposite side.

"Shall we begin?" Namor asks, obviously impatient to get started.

Stepping forward, you offer the Sub-Mariner your hand. With a shrug, Namor shakes it as the Wasp and Captain Marvel do likewise. Then you each go to your starting places. Turn to **47**.

132

"One bullet isn't going to stop me," you growl **153** at the mad HYDRA commander. Frozen with surprise by your failure to fall, your foe is incapable of dodging. You level him with a quick punch.

The HYDRA agent who helped you battle the other HYDRA agents has the presence of mind to offer you a clean cloth to press against the wound on your shoulder. A member of Freedom Flight fetches a first-aid kit and tapes the bandage in place. You may add 1 point to your Health.

Turn to **194**.

The pit is easily skirted once you are aware of **154** where the floor is solid and where it is not. From there on, the passage slopes down steadily. You halt suddenly.

"What is it?" Hoffman whispers.

"Shut off your flashlights," you order.

Up ahead, there is a different light spilling out to the passage where you stand, illuminating the objects of your quest. The rockets! Hundreds of them lined up in the passage! Hearing footsteps, the three of you duck behind the metal cylinders.

Ahead you hear a familiar voice, imperious and harsh—the Viper's voice.

"Keep up the transferences until you are no longer able. Don't you dare stop for a minor thing such as gunfire," the villainess orders.

Peeping from behind a missile, you see the infamous Viper speaking to two underlings struggling under the weight of one of the rockets. As the three figures head down the corridor, you and your companions stalk behind them, the sound of their footsteps muffling yours.

At a junction up ahead, Viper turns to the right and the men with the rocket go left. Motioning Agents Hoffman and Bronder to follow the rocket, you separate from them, turning right after the Viper.

Turn to **173**.

155 Your shield strikes Blacklash's head with a satisfying *thunk*, and Viper's hireling slides down the side of the rocket to the ground. You run forward cautiously, retrieving your shield and then checking on the condition of your foe.

He'll be okay, but he's out for this battle, you decide after checking his eyes, breathing, and pulse.

Turn to **28.**

156 You aim a powerful kick directly at the HYDRA commander's chest. Make a Fighting FEAT by rolling one die and adding the result to your Fighting ability. If the total is 13 or less, turn to **103.** If it is 14 or more, go to **161.**

157 "I'll take the bay side of the warehouse," you reply. "If Viper is planning on launching any rockets tonight, she's not going to do it where I am."

Hoffman grins. "It's such a lovely night; it's a shame you'll be stuck inside that dark, dank warehouse," he teases his partner.

"I hope it rains on you," she retorts.

As you slip around the sides of the warehouse with Agent Bronder, she explains that the SHIELD backup team is waiting two blocks away for her signal by walkie-talkie.

"Ken, er, Agent Hoffman and I usually check in every

quarter hour, or if we see anything suspicious."

"That will be fine," you agree. "If Viper's recruits show up inside, don't try anything without me," you order.

"No, sir. I'll wait till you get there to make Nitro explode," she assures you.

You watch as the SHIELD agent climbs the stairs to the loading dock and deftly picks the lock on the door at the top. After she slips inside the warehouse, you duck into the shadows by the stairs.

Minutes before the SHIELD agents' midnight walkie-talkie check-in is due, an eerie humming noise fills the air before you. Several yards away, three recognizable figures take shape. There is the unmistakable, ponytail-crested helmet of Blacklash, the muscular but aging form of Nitro, and, taller than either of these villains, a sleek steel gray rocket.

"They're here," you whisper into the walkie-talkie, suprrise in your voice. "Blacklash, Nitro, and a rocket. No Viper."

You wait a moment, trying to catch the drift of an argument Nitro and Blacklash are having.

"Why do I have to take orders from you?" Nitro growls.

"Because Viper trusted me, not you, with her plan," Blacklash snaps.

The rest of their words are carried away by the breeze. Then Nitro moves toward the warehouse, leaping up onto the loading dock.

"Nitro's heading for you, Bronder," you whisper. "I'm going to take him. Be ready with that gizmo of yours if he starts to vaporize."

Staying close to the shadows along the wall, you climb the steps onto the loading dock and poise yourself to charge the explosive man as he reaches the door Bronder disappeared behind.

To tackle Nitro, make an Endurance FEAT by rolling one die and adding the result to your Endurance ability. If the total is 7 or less, turn to **114**. If it is 8, 9 or 10, go to **36**. If it is 11 or more, proceed to **82**.

135

158 This is an easy shot, and you make it easily. Your red, white, and blue disk provides just enough momentum to knock the robot off balance.

Your mechanical foe crashes to the floor, its blades still hacking away, but it cannot follow you.

Add 1 to your Karma for defeating this formidable opponent without damaging it so much that it would be impossible to repair. Turn to **178**.

159 You ride with Director Chansler, Nick Fury, and Agents Bronder and Hoffman to Mobile Unit One—a truck trailer stationed directly across from the lower station of the Duquesne Incline. A dozen of Fury's field agents join you accompanied by Director Chansler's aide, Agent Lamb.

Agent Lamb displays an aging, yellowed map. "This is the layout of the coal mines under the hill before redevelopment. I can't vouch for how accurate it is now. We've stationed units at some likely looking exit points, places where we know the mines open into cellars or are being used as garages, that sort of thing." Pointing, she adds, "We've seen probable candidates for Viper hirelings exit at these two points and noted this secret exit within the Incline station itself."

Inspecting the map carefully, you trace out a path from Viper's hideout to a mine entrance that opens into a factory basement a few miles away. "Anyone come out through this route?"

"Not that we've noticed."

"That's the one I'll be taking."

"What?" Director Chansler asks in surprise.

"Give me half an hour, Nick. Once you attack she'll just use her teleporter. But I may stand a chance, if I sneak in alone, of grabbing her first."

"Sir," Agent Lamb protests, "like I said, I can't guarantee the accuracy of this map anymore, and especially not the safety of the mines."

Fury strokes his chin thoughtfully. "Will you take Agents Bronder and Hoffman with you?" he asks. "Then I wouldn't worry so much."

You glance at the two SHIELD officers' eager faces. They could slow you down; on the other hand, they could be of some help. If you decide to take them with you, turn to **22**. If you'd prefer to go alone, turn to **78**.

The last thing you see before you collapse is **160** Viper's vicious smile as she jabs you with something sharp.

Your first feeling on awaking is gratitude, for you are looking into the face of a friend, Nick Fury, director of SHIELD. You recognize your surroundings. You're in the emergency room of SHIELD's hospital complex.

"What—?" you begin, but find your chest is still wracked with pain.

"Save your breath, Cap," Fury suggests. "You're going to be fine. We got you here in plenty of time. Viper jabbed you with a couple of her snake-venom darts. We just gave you the anti-venom."

"Your agents—?" you whisper.

"Hoffman took quite a shock from Blacklash's necrolash. Hoffman's here, too. The doctors say he'll make it. Bronder was pinned under Blacklash's gravity bolo. She says Viper tried to kidnap you using Blacklash's teleporter ring, but the ring apparently couldn't carry two of you the distance to Viper's hideout.

"Blacklash didn't care for the idea of being left behind, since he could hear our sirens approaching, and while he and Viper were struggling for his ring, they dropped it. Bronder crushed it with Blacklash's bolo. Viper teleported out. Blacklash then made the mistake of freeing Bronder from the gravity bolo and trying to use her as a shield to get through our blockade. He ended up in the hospital, too."

"Viper's headquarters—?" you gasp. You can't rest, knowing Viper might still succeed.

"Blacklash gave us the location. We launched a raid right away, but Viper had fled already, with her personnel and some of the rockets. The best thing we can say is that she had to leave most of them behind."

Breathing suddenly feels easier. Viper is still free to brew up more poisonous schemes, but the immediate danger she posed to your country has passed.

Your adventure ends here. You may begin again, subtracting 1 point from your initial Health total and 1 from your Karma for what you have learned from this encounter with Viper.

161 Your kick knocks the HYDRA commander from his perch, and you leap down after him. Overhead you

can hear a rifle firing. Your foe is unconscious. Add 2 to your Karma points for defeating him.

Turn to **69**.

162 You lie on the ground, too stunned to rise. The mist that is Nitro in his vapor state drifts over to you. Groggy, you perceive it is coelescing back into Nitro's solid form.

"Good-bye, Captain America," Nitro sneers. A second pounding sweeps across your body, and your mind fades into darkness.

Subtract 10 from your Health points. You cannot subtract any of this damage from your Karma.

If you have 5 or fewer Health points remaining, turn to **54**. If you have 6 or more Health points, turn to **205**.

163 You aim a fist at Viper, but she dodges it expertly. The two of you circle one another warily. Turn to **115**.

164 "I won't do anyone any good if I collapse at a crucial moment," you decide. "I'll rest at least for today. Besides, there are some things I can take care of that don't require rough stuff."

You place a call to SHIELD, an organization that, like you, has fought Viper many times in the past. You are put through to SHIELD's director, Nick Fury.

"Hear you've been busy, Cap," the gruff former Army colonel greets you.

"Oh?"

"Got an intelligence report on my desk. You've been putting Viper's goons Nitro and Blacklash on the defensive. How'd you get into this?"

"Tip from the Constrictor, believe it or not. That's why I called, actually. He wouldn't tell me much. Now I'd like to get in touch with him and find out what else he might know. I don't suppose you have a clue as to his whereabouts?"

"I'll check it out. I think I might have someone on him as a matter of fact. I'll get back to you," Fury promises.

You spend the rest of the day at Avengers Mansion working quietly on your latest assignment for Marvel Comics—sketching for the *Captain America* comic book.

Later in the evening, Nick Fury calls you back. "This morning, Constrictor checked into the Liberty Hotel in Philadelphia, under his real name, Schlichting.

"That's where Freedom Flight's new headquarters is," you say.

"So it is," Fury replies.

"You seem to know a lot," you note.

"We're both after Viper, Cap. We were bound to run into each other eventually. Oh, and Cap, a warning. That rocket Viper's goons launched last night—"

"Yes?"

"She's got a lot more of those babies. She stole a whole shipment of them, so let's be careful out there."

"Yes, sir," you agree.

You feel much better after your day of relaxation. Add 5 back to your Health points. If you think you'd better continue with the doctor's advice and rest one more day, turn to **101**. If you think it would be better to drive to Philadelphia and check out Schlichting and Freedom Flight right away, turn to **91**.

165 The beam is blocked just at the moment it would have hit your partner, and Captain Marvel, now a brilliant silhouette of light, streaks toward you unharmed. Add 1 point to your Karma total for keeping your partner from injury.

Landing near you, Captain Marvel remains in her light form while she peers into the basket at your team's ball and shrugs. "No sweat," she says, slipping her shining hand into the glowing red light. As she draws the small sphere out, it changes from the red color of the inside of the basket to the white light her body is currently composed of.

"It must be made of unstable molecules," your partner guesses, changing herself and hence the ball back into matter.

"And only someone who can influence molecules could pick it up," you add, nodding.

"Care to do the honors?" the woman asks, handing you the ball.

Dashing through the remaining obstacles set in your path, you reach your final goal and toss the ball in the basket at the finish line nonchalantly. Captain Marvel whoops a cheer.

When the Wasp and the Sub-Mariner finally return with their ball, you and Captain Marvel are lounging against the wall.

The Wasp looks disgustedly at the computer's instant analysis of your score. "Perfect? Perfect! Where do you get off being *perfect?*" she chides.

"I had a lot of help," you explain, saluting your partner sharply.

"Perfect *and* modest. What a horrible combination."

"Perhaps you'll do us the honor of allowing us to learn more from you next week," Sub-Mariner suggests halfheartedly.

"I'll see if I can manage that," you agree.

Turn to **172.**

You and the HYDRA commander go tum- **166** bling off the edge of the tank. You use your foe to cushion your own fall. Overhead you hear rifle fire.

As you rise, the commander tries to do so as well, but

141

Agent Bronder, having dispatched her own opponent, lands a quick chop to the back of your foe's neck, putting him out cold.

Add 1 to your Karma points for helping to dispatch this HYDRA operative.

Turn to **69**.

167 You launch yourself feetfirst at the HYDRA leader. He spins toward you, but you hit him before he can aim his rifle. The weapon falls to the floor as your foe crashes into the desk.

In a moment you are on top of him.

"I surrender," the HYDRA leader groans.

Turn to **194**.

168 You lean against the cool mine wall and concentrate on listening. You imagine for a while that you hear the sounds of battle, but then there is nothing.

The next sound you hear awakens you. It is Nick Fury calling your name.

"Over here, Nick," you holler, alarmed at the echoes that ring about you.

Fury finds the pit and lowers a rope. Once you are raised, you sit with your rescuer for a few minutes to talk. He tells you that Viper did indeed get away with at least twenty-five more rockets, but that SHIELD captured the bulk of the missiles and now occupies Viper's secret base.

"I was so close. I got careless, Nick. Sorry," you say in crestfallen tones.

"We wouldn't have gotten this far without you, Cap. Don't take it out on yourself this way. You push yourself too hard sometimes. Lean on me, and we'll get out of here now."

As you limp out of the mines, using your friend as a crutch, you find yourself hoping that someday you'll get another chance at cornering the Viper.

"Don't worry, Cap. You will," Fury replies. "Knowing Viper and knowing you, it's a sure thing."

Your adventure ends here. You may begin again, subtracting 1 from your Health and 1 from your Karma for your losses.

You realize that you have used far too much **169** force as your shield shears through the robot's "neck." The disk bounces off of a wall and a hovering force field mechanism before it glides back towards you. You shudder to think what damage your throw could have done to a living thing, which is what the robot represents. Subtract 1 point from your Karma.

Still, you have managed to knock out the force field mechanism as well, freeing Captain Marvel from its dangers. Turn to **31.**

Your shield hits Blacklash in the legs, and he **170** crashes to his knees with a yelp of pain. Agent Bronder, not to be left out of things, uses the nozzle of the device she'd intended to capture Nitro with to smash Blacklash over the head.

The super villain slumps at her feet. "What do you know," the SHIELD agent comments, "it's a Blacklashbuster, too."

Agent Hoffman appears from the shadows and bends over Nitro's inert form. Rolling up the super villain's sleeve, Hoffman jabs him with an automatic hypodermic. "To be sure he stays unconscious until the energy-absorbing cuffs get here," he explains to you.

"Be sure and get their teleportation rings," you order the two of them.

Hoffman complies, finding and removing from Nitro's finger a wide band set with a large crystal that could enable him to disappear. "You have Blacklash's?" he asks as Bronder finishes tying the whip-wielder up with his own weapon.

Bronder holds up an identical ring. "This could be a free trip to Viper's hideout. I wonder if I could take her out with my Nitro-buster, too."

"I wouldn't recommend it," you reply. "She'd probably have an ambush waiting."

"Better put the ring down next to mine, Rambo," Hoffman suggests.

His partner complies with a sigh—not a moment too soon, for the rings both glow for a moment and then disappear. Turn to **147**.

171 The guard retreats from your flying attack, and you land at his feet. He smacks you over the head with what's left of his rifle butt. Subtract 2 points from your Health.

You grab your attacker's arms and toss him over the bar. Smashing into a mirror on the wall leaves your foe finally still. If your Health points have dropped to 0 or less, your adventure ends here.

If you can still go on, turn to **184**.

172 Once out on the street, you find that your earlier impatience has disappeared. The practice session has left you feeling relaxed, yet readier than ever to take on any crisis that comes your way.

In fact you feel so good that you decide to leave your

motorcycle parked at the Avengers Mansion and patrol on foot. You head south on Fifth Avenue, keeping your eyes and ears peeled for anything suspicious.

Turn to **214**.

The corridors you pass through are empty, **173** and the reason is obvious. Echoes of the noises of battle reverberate through them. SHIELD has begun its attack!

It's hard to tell in this maze of passages how close they are, you think. *But that's not my worry right now—Viper is.*

Viper, unaware you are stalking her and apparently unconcerned about SHIELD's attack, strides confidently and unhurriedly through her besieged complex. *She doesn't fear capture because she plans to teleport out,* you realize, *leaving most of her hirelings to fend for themselves.*

Viper enters what appears to be an information center. Numerous display screens cover one wall. She presses a button on a control panel. You are just about to announce your presence by throwing your shield at her, when you notice a swirling green glow on the largest screen in front of you. Something about that pattern disturbs you, frightens you even.

Viper turns around from the console, an evil grin spread across her face. "Welcome, Captain. I've been expecting you. I knew you would try sneaking up on me. Foolhardy."

You are about to taunt her by asking why she isn't already fleeing like the mad coward she is, but no words come out of your mouth. It's exactly as though you are in a dream where you need to scream, but can't.

"Entertaining little show, isn't it?" Viper asks, pointing to the screen. "People find it hard to tear their eyes away from it. I call it the serpent's stare. It's a variation of my old hypno-ray. I, of course, am immune to its effects."

You suspect that is not the complete truth. Viper must have some device that keeps her from falling prey to her 'serpent's stare.' You try to turn away from the screen, and then you learn you can't move either!

"I knew you were trying to sneak up on me," Viper brags. "I presume you're responsible for the SHIELD rabble fighting below us. You refuse to admit that everything you do is in vain."

Wallowing in your inability to reply, the Viper begins to lecture you. "I will not destroy your country. In the end, your nation's own weakness will be its downfall. I am just speeding up the process. You are so proud of this melting pot nonsense and America's supposed tolerance of ideas and respect for diversity. It's ironic, because that's what will destroy you in the end."

Viper pauses to push another button, and a list of names appears superimposed over the serpent stare pattern. "This is list of all those petty little factions stewing in distrust and hatred of their fellow man. See how long it is." The villainess holds her finger on a button and the list scrolls up the screen."

"You . . . trick them . . . with your lies," you manage to force these words from your lips.

Viper laughs shrilly. "Oh, you are stubborn. Despite the effort, you must defend your delusions. Don't you love the touch the rockets give this plan of mine. I had you in mind especially when I thought of the code name for my plan—the Rocket's Red Glare. All of these people have bought rockets," Viper says, waving her hand at the list of names on the screen.

"And the list of waiting customers is a thousand times as long. And after they've tasted first blood they'll be ready to find their own weapons. The rocket's red glare, the bombs bursting in air, will give proof through the night that your flag and all it stands for will CRUMBLE INTO DUST."

"Viper, you're mad!" you insist through clenched teeth.

"I've just given them what they want. Blood. It's time this precious nation of yours learned what the rest of the world has already learned—there is no liberty and justice for all. That's a myth the rich and powerful use to control the ignorant. There is only chaos and destruction!"

Whether the effect of the serpent's stare is diminished by the list of data sharing the screen or by the anger welling in you from listening to Viper's distorted and hateful perspective, you don't know for sure. But something gives you the strength to speak. "Only a few madmen will accept your way, Viper. Brave people all over the world struggle for the democratic principles this country was founded on. And the American people will never accept the mindless violence you wish to put in place of their freedom."

"You're a fool," Viper hisses, sneering and turning away from you, back to the information terminal. She is typing in orders to destroy her data banks.

You look at the list Viper is about to destroy. Names of all the people who have betrayed their faith in the very principles that shelter them, and your anger gives way to determination. Suddenly you feel less anxious, less frightened. As you concentrate on the names, you find that the serpent stare effect is decreasing!

If only I can escape this trap in time to stop Viper, you think.

You must summon all your willpower to fight the force of the serpent stare. Make a Psyche FEAT by rolling one die and adding the result to your Psyche ability. If the total is 7 or more, turn to **136**. If it is 6 or less, turn to **105**.

174 "Let's not waste any time, HYDRA scum," Agent Bronder says. "We want the location of Viper's headquarters. You might as well tell us now, because you will eventually."

"Never," the HYDRA agent sneers.

"But we're your only friends in the world right now, Commander Wright," Agent Hoffman asserts. "HYDRA does not forgive failure. And you have failed to capture Viper."

"I'm curious to know what made this man so sure that Viper would be here," you say, nodding toward the captive HYDRA agent.

"Viper does not make a move we do not know about. We know where her secret base is, and we will attack it," the prisoner brags.

"If you can find enough muscle, but you can't, can you? Viper's base is too well defended," Agent Hoffman quips. "That's why you were here—to try to capture her outside of it. Right? Right. Now answer Captain America's question," Hoffman orders, poking the HYDRA commander with his finger. "What made you think Viper would be here?"

"We've got a wiretap on Viper's phone lines. She made a rendezvous with Gress over the phone. She said she'd meet him at ten at Freedom Flight's headquarters," the HYDRA agent insists.

"But are you sure it was Kurt Gress?" you ask your captive. HYDRA Agent Wright looks confused.

"What Cap is trying to tell you," Agent Hoffman says, "is that there is another Mr. Gress—Aaron Gress, Kurt Gress's cousin."

"He's probably meeting Viper at the bombed-out Staten Island headquarters," you guess.

"Oh, Commander Wright," Agent Bronder chides, "you not only didn't capture Viper, you're not even in the same state as she is. Inefficiency. HYDRA *will not* be pleased."

The HYDRA agent squirms nervously, but does not reply.

"Doesn't HYDRA usually punish failure of that sort by eliminating the person responsible?" Agent Bronder continues, addressing her partner.

"According to all our intelligence reports." Agent Hoffman nods his head. "There was that HYDRA commander we fished out of the bay last week. And last month, the HYDRA accountant who made a mistake—they planted a bomb in his car."

"All right, all right!" the HYDRA commander cries out, shivering. "You swear you'll give me protection if I tell you where Viper's hideout is?"

"That's the deal, but we need that information like yesterday," Agent Bronder replies, drumming her fingernails on the desktop.

"How do I know you'll keep up your end of the deal?" Wright asks suspiciously.

"Would we lie to you in front of Cap here?" Agent Hoffman asks.

"It's in Pittsburgh. Under the Incline," the HYDRA agent blurts.

"What's the Incline?" Hoffman asks.

"Sort of a cable car, goes up the side of a hill. They have BIG hills in Pittsburgh," you explain, remembering a battle you fought there alongside the mighty Avengers.

"Are you interested in a change of scenery, Captain?" Agent Hoffman asks you. "We'd welcome your help in Pittsburgh, too."

"Thank you. I think I'd enjoy that. I hear the Viper hunting is good there this season."

Turn to **49**.

175 The computer presents several other obstacles that ordinarily you would consider minor—walls to vault, screens to climb—but your injury slows you down considerably.

Captain Marvel passes all the tests that confront her and reaches your destination way ahead of you, but the goal that the computer has chosen for your team is a cannonball weighing more than two hundred pounds—too heavy for your partner to lift. Upon reaching the basket yourself, you find your injury makes carrying the ball quite painful.

You manage to complete the exercise within the five minutes, but Wasp and Sub-Mariner win the bonus points for finishing first. They sit cockily on a bench, not bothering to try to slow you down any further. Their total score is greater than yours.

"You're right. I needed the practice," you tell the Wasp as you shake her hand in a show of good sportsmanship.

"I didn't say that," Jan objects.

"No, you're too polite and sneaky," you reply. "You were thinking it, though."

"You can get even next week if you have the time," Jan offers.

"I'll try to make the time," you agree. "And I'll do better for you next time, C.M.," you promise your partner.

"I know you will." Captain Marvel smiles,

undaunted.

"Come on, Cap," the Wasp insists. "Let's go tend that boo-boo."

The wound is bothering you, but so is the sense of urgency you have about finding the eye of the storm that you sense is brewing in the calm.

If you are willing to take the time to receive a little first aid before leaving the Avengers Mansion, turn to **119**. If you would rather just hit the streets and not worry about your injury, turn to **199**.

You cannot help thinking that you should **176** find out what HYDRA is up to. At the very least you can see to it that no innocents are injured in this assault, whatever it is. "I'd like to find out what this HYDRA assault is all about," you tell the SHIELD agents. "If you two are up to it."

"I always wanted to drive a tank," Agent Bronder grins.

"All right," Hoffman agrees. "But don't say I didn't warn you about her," he adds in an aside to you.

After driving for over an hour, the bus finally stops and the guard and the driver open the doors. You are in another warehouse, empty but for two monstrous tanks! Standing in front of these assault vehicles is the HYDRA commander in charge of this mission.

After everyone is given a rifle, the commander introduces himself and briefs you quickly. "We are going to attack a political headquarters called Freedom Flight. We couldn't care less about Freedom Flight, but they have a meeting this morning with a woman who calls herself Viper. She is to be captured alive, though not necessarily unharmed. Nothing else matters."

The bus driver displays a life-size poster of the Viper so that everyone can identify her if they see her, and then rolls it back up.

"So that's what this is all about," you think. "We'd better stick around, just in case HYDRA succeeds. We can't afford to let them capture Viper and acquire those

151

rockets she stole for themselves."

You signal Agents Hoffman and Bronder to continue with the undercover mission by following the HYDRA commander's order to get into the tanks.

Turn to **189**.

177 Satisfied that there's nothing seriously wrong, you decide to get right back to work. "I'll check out the rocket target site," you decide, heading your van back to Freedom Flight's former headquarters. Turn to **9**.

178 Continuing your journey across the room is no easy matter. Rubber bullets rain on your shield, nets descend to ensnare you, walls pop up from the floor. But sooner than you expected, you reach the basket holding your team's ball. Peering inside, you see that the ball is bathed in an eerie red light.

Using your shield, you try to scoop the ball out of the basket, but the small sphere seems to pass right through the disk. Suspecting that only Captain Marvel can get a hold on this phantom ball, you turn to inspect her progress.

Alternating her form from one type of energy to another, your partner is skillfully passing through numerous metal shields and evading force fields generated by hovering spheres. However, she's having a little trouble dodging an energy beam coming from a turret in the ceiling. The beam is dogging her flight path with frightening accuracy. Without hesitation, you toss your shield to deflect the beam away from Captain Marvel before she takes any damage from it.

To make this FEAT with your shield, roll one die and add the result to your Shield ability. Remember that you can spend Karma points on any roll to help ensure your success. If your total is 18 or less, turn to **102**. If it's 19 or more, turn to **165**.

You leap aside just as bullets catch you in the **179** shoulder and the leg. You must subtract 4 from your Health points.

It is hard to concentrate with the pain shooting through you. You know you must climb the ladder to the passenger seat, but you don't think you can make it. You can see Agent Bronder leaning out from the helicopter, reaching for you.

If your Health points are now less than 10, you must make an Endurance FEAT by rolling one die and adding the result to your Endurance ability. If the total is 8 or less, turn to **210**. If the total is 9 or more, or if you still have more than 10 Health points, turn to **74**.

I must end this quickly. A lightning quick **180** *attack should startle him and give me the edge I need.*

Make a Fighting FEAT. Roll one die and add the result to your Fighting ability. (Remember you can add Karma points if you like). If the total is 12 or less, turn to **85**, if it is 13, 14, or 15, go to **6**. If the total is 16 or more, proceed to **167**.

We can't let this man loose on this city in those **181** *tanks,* you decide. *He'll never succeed in capturing Viper that way, and he's liable to hurt someone. Time we took charge of his life and found out what he knows.*

"I want to capture the commander," you whisper to the SHIELD agents. "Be ready."

Agent Bronder is assigned to the tank with Commander Wright, and you and Agent Hoffman are assigned to the other. When all four of the other new HYDRA agents have climbed into the tanks, and you can no longer put off getting into your tank, you motion to Laura, who is standing on top of her tank with the commander and a veteran HYDRA agent.

Pretending to slip, she grabs for the commander to steady herself, but the man is either too cautious or callous, and he backs away from her. She is forced to grab onto the other veteran officer, and she and he tumble off the tank.

As the commander looks down at them with annoyance and shouts something unprintable, Agent Hoffman pushes the veteran officer on your tank over the edge, and you leap across to the other tank. Make an Agility FEAT by rolling one die and adding the result to your Agility ability. If the total is 11 or less, turn to **204**. If it is 12 or more, move on to **53**.

182 You cannot detect any flaws in the robot's armored body, and it's moving closer, preparing to mow you down like a weed. At any moment, you realize, one of the spearlike extensions from the thrashing machete arms may also come shooting out at you.

You weigh your options quickly. If you want to throw your shield with maximum force to be sure you stop the robot, turn to **8**. If you'd prefer to throw your shield with less force in hope of damaging the robot just enough to immobilize it, turn to **106**. Or if you'd rather just try to dodge past the robot, turn to **64**.

183 Your foot catches Nitro in the stomach, keeping him from exploding and knocking him off the loading dock. As he falls, Agent Bronder gives him a sharp rap on the back of his head with the nozzle of her complex-looking Nitro-buster, and Nitro crumples at her feet.

"You know, a club could have done the job just as easily," you note.

Bronder sighs. "Not if he'd gone boom."

You haven't time to be amused, though. You see that Blacklash is working frantically at the controls to the rocket, so you leap from the loading dock, over the SHIELD agent and her captive, toward the rocket.

But before you reach Blacklash, a SHIELD plasma beam, fired by Agent Hoffman, hits the villain at the rocket, knocking him to the ground. Blacklash tumbles away skillfully. Then a spectral glow encompasses him. When the glow fades, Blacklash is gone!

Turn to **26**.

Agent Bronder polishes off the other HYDRA **184** guard with a blow from the side of her hand. Before she lets him fall to the floor, she slides the rifle off from his shoulder as you retrieve your shield.

Make a Reason FEAT by rolling one die and adding the result to your Reason ability. If the total is 5 or less, go to **118**. If it is 6 or better, turn to **10**.

"Look, ya gotta trust me. It isn't a trap or **185** anything," the man's voice whines.

You are half convinced by his tone that it's a trap.

"Who is this?" you ask, but the caller hangs up.

Still tired from patrolling the city, and aching from the practice combat session at the Avengers Mansion, you decide not to check out this strange, anonymous tip tonight. Why would the caller insist on talking to you personally and then not tell you more than he did?

"He was probably a prankster," you decide. "But if he was laying a trap, he's going to find out he's not catching any captains tonight."

You leave the van parked behind Avengers Mansion, then slip into the mansion's back door and head for your room to spend the night in a real bed. After a night's sound sleep, you feel much better.

While you are eating breakfast, you note a curious short article in the newspaper. It appears that the tip you got last night was hotter than you thought. The article's headline reads, "Police Suspect Owner Started Warehouse Fire." According to the article, the owner may have been "playing around" with explosives.

You contact the Newark police and tell them about your tip, but it is so vague, you realize you can't be of much help to them. The police captain you speak to explains politely, "We appreciate your concern, sir, but we think we can handle this one without you. The case is pretty cut and dried."

You realize that you are being asked not to butt in. *Perhaps it is just a police matter,* you think. Still, you wonder why the tip came to you and not to the police. But you may never know the truth about the destruction of the Curtis Supply Warehouse.

Your adventure ends here. If you wish to begin again, you may do so, but you must reduce your initial Karma total by 2 for not taking the call of someone in need seriously.

156

The military jet commandeered by Nick Fury **186** lands at Pittsburgh's Allegeny County Airport at noon exactly. You are greeted at the gate by SHIELD's regional director for the area, Sylvia Chansler.

Turn to **17**.

Your charge knocks Blacklash off balance, **187** but he recovers with a backward somersault. Without bothering to rise to his feet, he activates his teleporter ring, which spreads a glowing light through the dim cellar, and then he is gone.

With a sigh, you help untangle Agent Bronder from the gravity bolo, and then the two of you check Agent Hoffman.

"He's breathing fine," Bronder notes. "What's that? Do you hear a humming?"

Spinning around, you note that the door to the secret office has been shut. You turn the doorknob, but the door doesn't budge.

Behind the door, you hear Viper's laughter. "Goodbye, Captain." The humming starts again and then stops.

You find that the ring you took from Viper is still in your belt pouch. *After he escaped, Blacklash must have teleported back with a second ring for Viper,* you surmise.

"The way she said good-bye was positively spooky," Agent Bronder says with a shiver.

"Yes, it was," you agree. "We'd better get out of here."

Together you drag Agent Hoffman up the metal ladder and out of the manhole, to the sidewalk.

Just as SHIELD cars begin pulling up in front of Freedom Flight's ex-headquarters, you feel the ground shake ever so slightly.

"She left a bomb in the secret room!" Bronder gasps.

You nod wordlessly.

Agent Hoffman begins to come around. "What happened?" he asks.

"My question exactly," a voice above you says.

Looking up, you see Nick Fury, director of SHIELD. You stand to shake hands.

"I thought we might be running into each other on this one," Fury says. "You okay, Ken?" he asks Agent Hoffman as Bronder helps her still-stunned partner to his feet.

"Just got a taste of Blacklash's stunning and electric personality," Hoffman moans.

"Blacklash was here?" Fury asks.

"Viper, too," you admit. "I'm sorry, Nick, but they both got away."

"And all we have to show for it is that two-bit ring from a crackerback jox," Agent Bronder jokes.

"Ring! You got a ring?" Fury asks excitedly.

You hold the ring up for his inspection.

"Viper's teleporter rings always disappear. We suspect she has a recall override on all of them."

"Maybe she forgot this one in all the excitement," Hoffman suggests.

"Dr. Arney!" Fury calls to a man, dressed in a white lab coat, who is standing in the door of a van crammed with electronic devices. The scientist takes the ring from you and slips it into a box with a cord leading to a computer.

"Please stand back, everyone," Dr. Arney requests. He flips a switch, and the box containing the ring glows, hums, and disappears.

After carefully monitoring the computer screen, Dr. Arney looks up with a big smile on his face. "Pittsburgh, Pennsylvania," he announces.

"That's where the ring went?" you ask.

"Yes. I'll have a more exact location within the hour," the scientist replies.

"All right!" Agent Hoffman cheers.

"Gonna' get me a big forked stick and go snake huntin' in Pittsburgh," his partner sings.

"Would you like to see this through with us, Cap?" Nick Fury asks.

"To the very end," you answer.

Turn to **39**.

158

You swerve aside just as Nitro and Blacklash **188**
both attack. Nitro explodes his fist in Blacklash's face
at the same instant that Blacklash tosses his bola over
his partner.

*There's nothing like watching close teamwork in
action,* you think with a grin. *Better finish the job on
Nitro before he panics and blows us all to kingdom
come.*

After knocking out the exploding man, you check on
his partner. Blacklash is out cold as well. You bind him
with his own whip.

"I hope whatever drug Viper gave Nitro wears off
before he comes to, or he'll escape anyway by blowing
up." You step back to survey your handiwork.

Make a Reason FEAT by rolling one die and adding
the result to your Reason ability. If the total is 4 or less,
go to **109**. If it's 5 or more, proceed to **11**.

You and Hoffman are assigned to a tank with **189**
two other new HYDRA agents and one veteran. Agent
Bronder and the rest, including the commander, climb
into the other tank.

The tanks rumble out from the warehouse and down
the street. You cannot see where you are going, but you
realize anyone outside the tank would notice you a mile
off. *What does HYDRA hope to achieve by this heavy-
handed approach?* you wonder.

You cannot resist asking the HYDRA officer in
charge, "Wouldn't it be better to sneak up on Viper?"

The HYDRA agent looks at you as though you are a
fool. Patronizingly, he explains, "Once we capture her

we need these tanks to be sure she cannot escape us, or be wrested from us by the authorities. See?"

You answer, "Yes, sir," but what you are really thinking is, *Only a fool would think Viper would stand around waiting while a tank lumbers toward her. She's mad, but not deaf.*

Several minutes later, the tank stops and you and Hoffman are ordered to get out. Outside, you find you are in an alley behind a row of townhouses. The HYDRA officer points to a door, and someone in the tank fires a missile at it, smashing it in. You are all but convinced that the HYDRA commander is mad, too.

"Go through there," he orders. "Herd everyone you see into the front room. Don't let anyone escape."

You realize you'd better not let anyone past you, since the tank would only fire upon them. Fortunately, no one resists your invasion, and you and Agent Hoffman soon find yourselves in the living room of the townhouse, guarding five men and two women while the HYDRA commander shouts questions at them. The front wall of the room has been smashed in by the tank Agent Bronder is in.

"Where is she?" the commander barks.

"Who?" the oldest prisoner, a middle-aged man, asks, looking confused.

"Don't act stupid! Viper—where is she? We know she's here, Gress. We heard you arrange a meeting with her for this exact time to buy one of the rockets. You will hand over Viper, the rocket, and the money you were going to pay her, now!"

"I don't know what you're talking about," the prisoner protests, clearly bewildered.

The HYDRA leader knocks the man back with the butt of his rifle. "Don't make me angry!" he shouts. "I shoot people when I'm angry."

Now you are sure Commander Wright is cracking up. Even if Viper had been here, which does not seem likely, she'd be long gone by now.

"I think you're mistaken," you say in a quiet voice. "Besides, this has gone on long enough."

Before you lose the element of surprise that your comment has caused, you launch yourself at the HYDRA commander. Make a Fighting FEAT by rolling one die and adding the result to your Fighting ability. If the total is 12 or less, go to **7**. If it is 13 or 14, turn to **128**. If it is 15 or more, proceed to **97**.

The Viper hangs up on you, and you lay the **190** phone receiver back down on its cradle.

"Apparently Nitro was correct," you announce. "That was Viper calling for someone named Gress. She'll be here in ten minutes with a rocket."

"The game's afoot," Agent Bronder cheers, her eyes sparkling with exitement.

"That doesn't give us much time," Hoffman mutters.

"Sorry," you apologize. "She wouldn't be put off, and we can't lose her now."

Agent Hoffman nods in agreement. "I'm going to put in a call for backup," he says, reaching for the phone.

You spy a slip of paper under the phone and pick it up to examine it. "This might explain why Mr. Gress isn't here to answer his phone; he's probably paying his phone bill," you state, showing the SHIELD agents the paper. It's a cut-off notice for a Mr. Aaron Gress from the phone company, demanding payment before resumption of services.

"I wonder how Mr. Gress intended to buy a rocket if he can't even afford to pay his phone bill," Agent Bronder murmurs.

"Viper is selling them cheap," you point out. "This one's going for only five grand."

"Figures. The rockets didn't cost her much to steal,

and she's making sure just about anyone can afford one," Bronder notes.

"No doubt," you agree. "How much chaos she can spread would be her main motivation, not profit. Let's see what's back here, shall we?" you suggest, pointing to the door in the back of the room.

Drawing her weapon, Agent Bronder covers you as you push open the door. Behind is a large, cavernous second basement with empty crates and barrels stacked within. Against one wall a metal ladder leads up to a manhole cover. There are no lights in the room.

"This would be a good place to hide and wait," you propose. "We can block the secret door into the other basement."

Agent Hoffman joins the two of you. "I've called for backup, but they won't make it here in time. Aaron Gress, by the way, is a member of Freedom Flight; he's a Latverian political refugee, and his cousin is Freedom Flight's founder. I presume you have a plan?" he asks you.

"Yes. Slide that manhole cover over a few inches so a little light shines in, and then go lie down at the bottom of that ladder and play possum. That should attract their attention when they arrive."

"They? You don't think Viper will come alone?" Hoffman asks.

"No. She'll bring someone to do the dirty work."

Agent Hoffman follows your orders and positions himself while his partner jams the secret door mechanism so it cannot be opened.

You wait anxiously behind a stack of crates in the shadowy secret cellar. Crouching next to you, Agent Bronder keeps switching her plasma-beam weapon from hand to hand in nervous anticipation.

"Don't jump the gun, young lady," you warn. "Viper may bolt at the first sign of deception."

"She wouldn't be so tough without that lousy teleporter," Bronder sniffs.

"You're wrong about that," you whisper. "It was her dangerous cunning that got her that teleporter."

You do not have to wait much longer for the now-familiar sound of Viper's teleporter delivering someone into the smaller room.

You hear Blacklash's voice ask, "Well, where is he?"

"Check out there," Viper's voice commands.

The door into the room you are in swings wide open, and now Blacklash is in sight, but you remain frozen.

"There's someone lying at the foot of the ladder," Blacklash whispers.

"Well, go check it out," Viper says in a bored tone. "Perhaps he took a tumble. See if the money is on him."

Blacklash crosses the cellar floor, leaving the doorway unguarded. Moving as one, you and Agent Bronder step out from behind the crates, you toward the open door and Bronder toward Blacklash.

The dimness provides a certain amount of camouflage for your ambush, but you know that silence is absolutely crucial. Make an Intuition FEAT by rolling one die and adding the result to your Intuition ability. If the total is 12 or less, go to **88**. If the total is 13 or more, proceed to **111**.

You have no idea how much time has passed **191** when you awaken, still a prisoner, still strapped to a table. Blacklash is in the room with you, or rather, Mark Scarlotti, for the criminal is dressed in ordinary clothing and not in his Blacklash costume. Apparently he's just given you an injection to bring you around.

Whatever the shot was, it has given you a feeling of strength and clear-headedness. Surreptitiously you test your metal bonds. *I might just slip out of the strap holding my right wrist to the table—if I'm willing to leave some skin behind,* you think.

Scarlotti lays your shield on top of your chest and drops a dandelion on top of the disk.

"I'm fantasizing about your funeral, Captain America," the man says, giggling. "But don't worry. Viper still wants you alive. She's going to get you to help sell her rockets."

"She's mad, Scarlotti, if she thinks she can make me do anything of the sort." Secretly, you are grateful for the cover your shield provides as you try tugging your hand upward.

"Oh, you'd be surprised. She has the most impressive assortment of mind-altering drugs I've ever seen."

"And it would seem you've been into them," you state, noting his dilated pupils and quirky movements.

"A little reward for capturing you."

"I see. More poppy derivatives. You're a bigger fool than I thought, Blacklash."

"I captured you. Just remember that, Flagman. I captured you all by myself."

"You're mind's going already, Scarlotti," you sniff. "You had help from Nitro, remember?"

"Nitro, hah! This scam's better off without him. I'm glad he's gone."

He left, hmm? Couldn't take Viper's madness maybe? You wonder if it's too much to hope that Viper's organization may already be crumbling—eaten away by her courtship with nihilism, drugs, and insanity.

"That old fool just couldn't recognize Viper's genius."

"I think you admire her because she's one of the few people around who is more unstable than you are, Scarlotti," you taunt.

"You just wait, Captain Nowhere," Blacklash shouts. "You'll see. People will spit on you when Viper finishes."

You take advantage of Blacklash's distracted agitation and give your hand one final jerk. Before you have a chance to feel the pain caused by scraping the skin off your hand, you grab at your shield so it won't slip to the ground.

With your other arm and both legs still bound, you know you will have only one shot or Blacklash will summon help. Make a Shield FEAT by rolling one die and adding the result to your Shield ability. If the total is 20 or less, turn to **141**. If it is 21 or more, turn to **5**. Remember you can spend Karma on your die roll.

164

I'd better check out Schlichting's story, you **192**
decide. *After all, he has good reason to want the Viper
captured. It'll keep the whole world, and especially
him, safe. I'll go alone, though, in case it's a false alarm.
Then I won't be wasting anyone's time but my own.*

You patrol the city until dusk and then return to
Avengers Mansion for a quick bite to eat. Then, in case
you need it later, you stow your Harley-Davidson
motorcycle in the back of your customized van, which
is parked behind the mansion headquarters.

*I should try to get a little rest before tonight's stake-
out,* you think. You lie down on the built-in cot in the
rear of the van, but not knowing what Viper is up to
makes you too tense to sleep. Finally, after tossing rest-
lessly for an hour, you give up.

Turn to **14**.

As a bright light flashes from the tank, you **193**
swerve the car as quickly as you are able without running off the road into a ditch. The car is hit anyway. A
mortar shell tears through the passenger side, but the
vehicle still functions, and you speed past the tank,
knowing it cannot catch up with you.

You glance at Laura Bronder beside you. She is
unconscious and bleeding from a cut on her head.
Steering the car with one hand, you cradle her head in
your lap and apply direct pressure to the wound to stop
the bleeding. You know that if you stop, HYDRA will
catch up to you.

A police car finally cruises up beside the Cadillac and pulls you over. Flashing your Avenger's ID, you convince the officer in charge to help you get your companion to a hospital.

Two days later, Agent Bronder is taken off the critical list. You visit her in the hospital with her partner, Ken Hoffman. After saying hello, you hand her a bouquet of violets.

"My favorites," she whispers.

"Your partner told me," you confess.

"I don't feel like I deserve them," she sighs. "Colonel Fury told me that while I was unconscious, Viper fled her headquarters and HYDRA got most of her rockets anyway. I should have given you the location of her secret base while we were making our getaway so you wouldn't have had to wait for me to come to."

"We were both a little preoccupied," you console her. Besides, Nick Fury told me that it would be a lot easier tracking the rockets from HYDRA than finding out who Viper would have sold them to."

"Still," Bronder says, "it's a lot more work. And you went to so much trouble getting me away from HYDRA."

"I wouldn't consider it time wasted," you say.

"Try to look on the bright side, Laura," her partner advises. "We kept HYDRA from occupying Viper's old hideout, since it wasn't so secret anymore, thanks to you. And you gave us more dirt on HYDRA than we've accumulated in the last year. Not only that, but we captured HYDRA's secret base, using your information. We got that tank, too."

"I want that stuffed and hung over my mantle," Bronder growls. Then, more seriously, she adds, "I wanted to catch the Viper so bad."

"Me, too," you admit. "And we still might someday. So get better."

"Yes, sir," Bronder salutes you.

Your adventure has come to an end. When you play again, subtract 2 from your initial Karma total for what you've lost and what you've learned.

You hold onto the HYDRA leader firmly while
the double agent who aided you handcuffs him. Add 2
to your Karma points for assisting in the capture.

"Just who are you?" you ask your helper.

"Ken Hoffman. SHIELD special agent, sir," the man
replies, removing the mask that is part of his HYDRA
uniform.

"What's SHIELD?" Mr. Gress asks as you help him
up from the floor.

"Supreme Headquarters International Espionage
Law-enforcement Division," you explain. "He's one of
the good guys."

"That's debatable," a woman's voice retorts. The
speaker, also dressed in a HYDRA uniform, is standing
in the doorway.

"That's my partner, Laura Bronder—also an undercover agent for SHIELD," Hoffman explains. "You
should talk," he chides the woman. "Look what you did
to these nice people's wall with that tank. Do you know
you're a menace?"

"Sorry about that folks," Agent Bronder says, shrugging. "But I was undercover, and I had to do what
HYDRA ordered. If you would all step outside, our
administrator, Mr. Johnson, will debrief you and discuss recompense with you."

The Freedom Flight members file out of their own
headquarters.

"Director Fury said we'd probably run into you on
this one, Cap," Agent Hoffman comments, turning
back your way. "He says you and Viper go way back."

"I've fought her before," you say, nodding. "But why
is HYDRA so anxious to get her?"

"She stole our rockets!" the captured HYDRA commander accuses.

"You mean the rockets she stole before you could do
it yourselves," Agent Hoffman laughs. "They're Uncle
Sam's rockets. She got over six hundred of them."

You shake your head, amazed at the number and
gravely concerned about the damage Viper could cause
with them. "Those rockets must be recovered."

"That's our job," Agent Bronder says. She and her partner sit down on either side of the captured HYDRA leader.

Turn to **174**.

195 Unable to help Captain Marvel in time, you watch as she is struck by the energy beam. She transforms back to matter in midair and immediately crashes to the floor. As you rush toward her, she rises awkwardly.

"You get the license plate of that truck?" she jokes.

"Are you okay?" you ask.

The energy-transformer nods, then adds ruefully, "It looks as though we've lost the bonus."

The Wasp flies by with a ball in her hands.

"We still have time to finish," you point out, urging Captain Marvel on.

Reaching the basket again, this time with your partner, you watch as she bypasses the heat field by changing herself into light energy. As she draws the ball out, it shines just as she does.

"The ball must be made of unstable molecules," Captain Marvel explains, transforming herself and the ball back into matter once more.

"And only someone able to alter molecules could get a hold of it," you say with a nod.

You reach for your shield and head back to the opposite wall. The Wasp and the Sub-Mariner have already dropped their ball in their finish line basket, so you lose the bonus for finishing first. Your team's total score is slightly higher, however, due in part, you realize, to the fact that you got past your obstacles without causing extensive damage to the room or its defenses.

Namor scowls with annoyance at the red-ant stings he received trying to reach for his team's ball. "You must teach me how to tell those insects to get out of my way," he says to Jan.

"You have to ask them very politely," the woman explains. "Communication with ants requires exceptional diplomacy."

"I enjoyed the session," you say. "Thanks for asking me."

"I'm glad," Jan answers. "If you have time, we can do it again next week. Then Namor and I will have a chance to get even."

"I'll try to fit it into my schedule," you promise. "Good afternoon, ladies . . . Namor," you say as you head for the door.

Turn to **172**.

You stop to consider for a moment why there **196** would be a staircase going up. The entrance you took was rather high up the side of the mountain, and the passages haven't sloped down much. If you continue climbing like this you'll end up above ground again.

Everything has that polished look that only a technological genius such as the Viper could have created. You flip off your flashlight and it all becomes clear. The first fifteen steps vanish in the darkness, but the ones that follow them give off their own eery light. You climb the lower steps to investigate more closely.

You touch the first glowing step with your shield only to learn that the strange step has no substance. *It's a holographic projection,* you realize. *A trap of Viper's, all right,* you mutter. Feeling carefully, you discover that the false stairs go over a pit trap that must be quite deep. You carefully skirt the edges. Turn to **100**.

Viper fires just as your shield is about to **197** strike her. Her weapon's power blast keeps the disk from smashing into her at full force, but the shield still

travels with enough momentum to knock the weapon from her grip.

Viper glares at you, her attractive face distorted by hatred. "You will pay for your interference, Captain," she snarls.

You leap forward to grab her, but she has already operated her teleporter ring. A glowing light surrounds her and she disappears. Turn to **127**.

198 "A little background first. . ." Fury begins. "Viper wasn't the only one who wanted this shipment of rockets. HYDRA was after them as well, for some scheme of their own."

"But Viper snapped them up right from under HYDRA's nose," Hoffman continues, "so Viper is persona non grata with them—not that they've been on especially good terms with her since she left HYDRA."

"Our intelligence division reports that HYDRA knows the location of Viper's secret base, but the would-be world conquerors are currently too under-manned to take it by force," Bronder adds. "HYDRA has been trying to catch Viper outside of her headquarters—to teach her a 'lesson,' and more notably, to get her to hand over the rockets."

"So you need to get into HYDRA to find out the location of Viper's secret base," you guess.

"Precisely," Fury replies. "And HYDRA has opened the door for us to do so. According to one of our informants, HYDRA is holding massive recruitment drives."

"Looking for muscle to storm Viper's base?" you ask.

"That's what we figure," Agent Hoffman says, nodding. "We thought we'd apply as hired thugs. HYDRA will take anyone at this stage, including costumed super villains."

"We've got another costume you can wear to hide your own, if you want to join Ken and Laura on this mission," Fury explains.

"What are we waiting for?" you ask.

Turn to **76**.

'No, thanks, Jan," you insist. "It's just a **199** flesh wound. I have to be going now."

"Suit yourself, but take it easy, okay?"

"Yes, ma'am," you agree as you wave good-bye to your fellow Avengers. Taking the elevator up to the main floor, you head out to the street.

Turn to **77**.

The HYDRA agent is completely alert, and he **200** knocks your shield away with his rifle. As he starts to aim his weapon, though, it cracks into two pieces, destroyed by the force of your adamantium disk.

Vaulting over the bar you leap at the guard. Make a Fighting FEAT by rolling one die and adding the result to your Fighting ability. If the total is 12 or less, turn to **171**. If it is 13 or more, turn to **30**.

201 "That's where the rocket came from? Who were they launching it against?" you ask.

"Tell him, Scarlotti," Agent Bronder orders Blacklash, addressing him by his real name.

"I don't answer to dames," Blacklash sneers.

"You want to step outside, Scarlotti?" Bronder challenges.

"Down, Laura. We may need him in one piece," Agent Hoffman warns.

"I'd be more polite, if I were you, Blacklash," Fury advises. "I trained Agent Bronder myself, and my money is on her."

"You took orders from Viper," you point out to Blacklash. "She's a woman."

"She paid well," Blacklash says, grinning.

"For what?" you ask.

With a shrug, Blacklash sits back and starts to talk. "We sell these rockets to political organizations—terrorists mostly. But there aren't enough of them around in this country, so we've started convincing less extremist groups that they need them, too. If there's one paranoid or violent apple in the bunch, Viper knows how to find him. The group uses the rocket and then their enemy has got to have one to use in retaliation. Our business increases."

"We're talking civil warfare here, Blacklash!" you snap. "How could you be a part of this madness?"

"I told you, Viper pays well. Besides what do I care if a few crazies blow each other up?"

"Tell Director Fury and Captain America what you told me about this rocket," Agent Hoffman orders Scarlotti.

"Viper tried to sell it to this guy—Curtis. He owns this warehouse. He belongs to some kook organization called the People's Choice of Latveria that supports Victor Von Doom—that fascist guy who rules Latveria, you know?"

"Is Doom involved in this, too?" you ask in surprise, aware that Lord Doom of Latveria is another would-be world conqueror.

"Nah!" Scarlotti answers. "He doesn't have anything to do with American peasants, not even the ones who are for him like this Curtis guy. Anyway, this Curtis won't bite. He insists he's not a violent man. So Viper says to make it look like Curtis's PCL used the rocket anyway—on their rivals—some anti-Doom group called Freedom Flight. Their headquarters is on Staten Island. We were supposed to launch the rocket from Curtis's property and then blow up his warehouse to teach him a lesson about being such a chicken. That was Nitro's job."

"You're such scum, Scarlotti," Agent Bronder whispers.

Unperturbed, the villain just grins.

Blacklash sits up straight. "What are you talking about? You got nothing on me but possession of this dumb rocket, and you know it, SHIELD boy."

"Don't be stupid, Scarlotti," Nick Fury advises. "Viper has declared her intention to overthrow our government on numerous occasions. You don't think she's selling these rockets for her health, do you?"

Blacklash seems unable to reply. He looks confused.

"Think, Blacklash," you urge. "If Viper creates enough chaos with these rockets, if the violence gets out of hand, it will be that much easier for her to destroy us. Have you ever seen a citywide riot? That's what it will be like all over this country if Viper goes on peddling these weapons."

"You don't want to be responsible for that, do you,

Scarlotti?" Agent Hoffman asks. "Tell us where she is."

Blacklash shifts uneasily. "Pittsburgh," he croaks. "Under the Incline."

"The what?" Hoffman asks.

"The Incline," you echo, remembering it was the scene of a battle you once fought in alongside the mighty Avengers. "It's a cable car that goes up the hill. They've got big hills in Pittsburgh."

"Big snakes, too," Bronder adds.

"Hoffman and Bronder will be arranging the raid on Viper's hideout. Would you care to give them a hand, Cap?" Nick Fury offers.

"Sure. I'd like that," you reply.

Turn to **186**.

202 Suspecting that the red glow surrounding the ball may come from some dangerous energy source, you decide to wait for Captain Marvel, who can easily foil such a trap by transforming herself into the same kind of energy. You spot her form, now changed to living light, as she swoops down on your shield.

Merely by willing it, she takes on her own material form as she calls out, "Special Delivery, Cap," and tosses you your shield.

Catching the shield deftly, you watch as your partner streaks past several force fields generated by hovering spheres. Then she changes into an energy form able to pass through the metal shields dropping down from the ceiling. You become concerned when a particularly well-trained energy beam shooting from a turret in the ceiling starts closing in on Captain Marvel. Instinctively you toss your shield to deflect the beam away from her.

To make this FEAT with your shield, roll one die and add the result to your Shield ability. If the total is 18 or less, turn to **102**. If it is 19 or more, turn to **165**.

You grab Viper's arms and get a firm grip **203** about both of her slender wrists. Even after you have yanked her teleporter ring from her finger, she does not surrender gracefully. She breaks free a moment later and tries to slam you in the chest with her foot.

"Enough of this," you mutter. You level Viper and all her rage with one blow to the back of her neck. She slumps in your arms, defeated. Turn to **215**.

You land easily on the roof of the other tank, **204** but the HYDRA commander grapples with you to keep from being pushed off the edge of the tank. His strength is too close to your own for you to just shove him over.

You break free of the HYDRA commander's hold on your sleeves and back away. *I have to get this man under control,* you realize.

If you decide to charge, taking both you and your foe over the edge of the tank, turn to **20**. If you'd rather launch a karate kick at him, go to **156**.

You awaken to another booming sound. You **205** can see the warehouse's corrugated walls sagging on their supports and its roof caving in. A mist floats over the warehouse and then swiftly drifts out of sight across the bay.

Judging from my uniform's tattered condition, you think, *Nitro must have blown up on me again, before he took out the warehouse.*

"Are you all right?" a voice whispers from behind a parked truck trailer.

You rise slowly, wincing in pain as you go to and

investigate the sound. Crouching low in fear is a pudgy, elderly man in a business suit.

"I've been better," you answer. "Who are you?"

The man rises to his feet. "Steven Curtis," he says. "That was my warehouse."

"What happened to the rocket?" you ask, noting its absence.

"They launched it," Mr. Curtis answers.

"Why did Viper do this, Mr. Curtis?"

At Viper's name, Mr. Curtis starts. "You know about her?" he whispers.

"Yes, sir," you reply. "But more importantly, what do *you* know about her?"

"She threatened to destroy me."

"Why, Mr. Curtis?" you persist.

"She wanted me to buy one of those rockets, but I refused. I'm not a violent man, Captain America. You must believe me. She said if I wouldn't live by the rocket's red glare, I would die by it. She's trying to frame me."

The defeated tone of the warehouse owner's voice convinces you he is telling the truth. "But why would Viper try to sell you a rocket, Mr. Curtis?"

It seems unbelievable to imagine this mild-mannered little man using such an instrument of destruction.

"Because I'm the founder of the PCL. She tried to convince me that I needed one because Freedom Flight has one. I didn't believe her."

"What's the PCL? And what is Freedom Flight?"

"PCL stands for People's Choice of Latveria. We support Lord Doom's government."

"Victor Von Doom?" Your head swims from the contradictions. Besides being the ruler of Latveria, Doom is himself a would-be world conqueror. In your opinion, Doom is mad and quite dangerous. Why would someone like Mr. Curtis support him?

"Oh, I know what you're thinking, Captain," Mr. Curtis goes on. "You super heroes have often fought against Doom, and you may have been right. But what-

176

ever you think of him, he's the best leader Latveria has had ever. He has been good for the people. I am a U.S. citizen now, but I was born in Latveria, and it was a terrible place before Lord Doom took over. The aristocracy walked all over the peasants. Things have changed for the better."

You consider the wisdom of Mr. Curtis's words. Latveria does not have the benefit of American-style democracy, yet it is better off than many other small nations. "But what about Freedom Flight?" you ask again.

"They're a group of refugees who oppose Lord Doom. They want to bring down his government. Their headquarters is on Staten Island, just south of here, across the bay. I think they are wrong, Captain, but I would never have done them any harm."

"Then Blacklash and Nitro launched the rocket at Freedom Flight?"

Mr. Curtis nods. "Then they blew up my warehouse to get even with me for not buying their rocket."

"I want you to tell the police what you told me, Mr. Curtis."

"They won't believe me."

"I'll back up your story with what I discover. But I have to go now."

You drive out to Staten Island, traveling just within the speed limit, but by the time you arrive, Freedom Flight's headquarters is a blazing inferno. Two fire-fighting crews are already on the scene, battling the fire.

"Is there anyone in there?" you ask a police officer who is helping to keep back a crowd of curious onlookers.

"Well, that's the miracle of it," the policeman tells you. "You see, these Freedom Flight people moved to a new headquarters in Philadelphia this morning. They say they were too close to that Latverian embassy for comfort, that they were afraid of reprisals from the Latverian Secret Police. I heard they lost their lease. Anyway, as far as we know, the building is empty. No one's been hurt. Does that sound like luck or what?"

"Sounds like 'or what,' " you reply, wondering if Viper's plan has been thwarted by a twist of fate, or if this was part of her plan. *This would be a good way to convince Freedom Flight to buy a rocket, and you can't sell anything to the dead, so maybe she warned them. It's so hard to figure out her twisted schemes,* you think, shaking your head.

"Are you all right, sir?" the police officer asks you.

You see that the man is inspecting your tattered uniform and bruised face.

"You look like you've been in quite a tussle," the officer notes.

"I suppose so," you reply vaguely.

"Maybe you should see a doctor," he suggests.

"I'll consider it, sergeant. Thank you."

You return to your van, which is parked a few blocks from the burning building, and collapse wearily onto the cot, exhausted from your battle and the day's confusion. When you awaken late the next morning, you feel a little better.

Add 2 back to your Health point total, but you are still bruised and sore. If you decide to take the time to visit a doctor as the police officer suggested, turn to **124**. If you are so concerned about the damage Viper and her goons may do that you don't think you can afford to take time to see a doctor, turn to **42**.

206 You tuck into a roll, and the bullets bounce off of your shield. With a leap, you reach the ladder and climb into the chopper. Agent Bronder lifts off the roof of HYDRA's secret base. Turn to **89**.

With a supreme effort of will, you remain **207** standing despite your wound. The HYDRA commander backs away from you with his rifle aimed at your middle. He leaps out the hole that his tank made in the front wall of the building.

You are about to jump down after him when a shot rings out and your quarry falls over. He lies in the street, unmoving.

"Sniper fire! Stay back!" someone shouts, tugging on your shirt. Backing away from the hole, you realize that the warning came from the HYDRA agent who helped you battle the other HYDRA agents.

"Who are you? What's going on?" you demand.

The HYDRA agent pulls the HYDRA uniform mask off his head. "Ken Hoffman, SHIELD special agent, sir," the man introduces himself. "Offhand, I'd guess that a HYDRA sniper just shot the commander."

"Why?" you ask.

Agent Hoffman shrugs. "Probably because he knew too much. HYDRA couldn't risk his capture. Also because he failed to capture Viper. The sniper will be long gone. Can I put something on that wound for you?" the SHIELD agent offers.

One of the Freedom Flight members brings Agent Hoffman a first-aid kit so he can bind your wound. Add 1 to your Health points. Add 1 to your Karma, too, for helping to keep the members of Freedom Flight safe.

"What is SHIELD? Who is this Viper woman? And what were you doing pretending to be one of those men?" Kurt Gress asks Agent Hoffman as the SHIELD agent tends to your injury.

"SHIELD stands for Supreme Headquarters Intelligence Espionage Law-enforcement Division," Agent Hoffman explains. "Viper is a very wicked lady who's stolen a very large shipment of rockets from Uncle Sam. HYDRA is furious, since they wanted to steal these same rockets for themselves. We had a lead that HYDRA knows where Viper's hideout is. So we joined HYDRA undercover to find out what we could—'we' is me and my partner, who should be outside somewhere.

Anyway, HYDRA is holding off attacking Viper only until they can get enough manpower. In the meantime, they tried this stunt. Now, I have a question for you, Mr. Gress. Do you have any idea why HYDRA thought Viper would be meeting you here?" the SHIELD agent asks.

Mr. Gress shakes his head slowly.

"Perhaps Viper was meeting the other Mr. Gress," you suggest. "—Aaron Gress. Do you know what your cousin's unfinished business in New York was, Mr. Gress?" you ask.

"You've figured it out, Cap," a voice from the doorway announces. "Aaron Gress was trying to buy a rocket." The speaker is none other than Nick Fury, director of SHIELD. "Would you ladies and gentlemen please step into the hallway so Administrator Johnson can debrief you?" Fury requests, waving the members of Freedom Flight out of the room.

As soon as Mr. Gress and his people file out, Fury shuts the door behind them. "Are you okay?" he asks you, noting your bandage.

"Fine," you reply. "Just a flesh wound. I take it you stopped Aaron Gress from getting his rocket?"

"Well, not exactly," Fury admits. "He didn't have the cash to buy one, even though Viper is selling them really cheap."

"I don't think she's interested in the money," you assert. "She's only interested in how much chaos she can spread getting people to use the rockets. Am I right?"

"Bull's-eye," Fury nods. "Still, she's not giving them away. It cost her something to steal them, and she's got other expenses. When Gress couldn't show her the money, she refused to show him a rocket. There was some sort of argument, and Blacklash started to rough up Gress. Gress shot Blacklash with a gun he'd kept hidden. Viper got away, but we have Blacklash."

"Then we can can find out the location of Viper's hideout from him," Agent Hoffman says.

"I'm afraid not, Ken," Fury answers. "Blacklash is in

intensive care and probably won't be able to talk for a few days. Viper will have moved by then. We captured Nitro this morning, but he couldn't tell us a thing. Viper kept him completely in the dark. We were really relying on you and Bronder to break into HYDRA's computer. Where is Agent Bronder, anyway?"

"Laura!" Agent Hoffman gasps. "She was with the HYDRA sub-commander."

"We didn't capture any sub-commanders," Fury says in a tight voice.

"Laura must be escaping back to the HYDRA secret base with him, trying to stay undercover. She hasn't had enough time yet to break HYDRA's computer codes and learn where Viper's hideout is. I'll bet she's gone back to do it."

"Without backup?" Fury growls.

"Well, you know how Laura is, sir," Agent Hoffman answers meekly.

"Yes. Foolish and headstrong."

"Something I can help with, Nick?" you offer.

"How are you at rounding up stray sheep?" Fury asks. "We've got to get Bronder away from HYDRA."

Turn to **108.**

You catch the HYDRA agent in a headlock. **208** He struggles fiercely, but he cannot shake your hold. Agent Bronder injects something into an artery in his throat with a tiny needle hidden in her ring, and he collapses.

"The old needle-in-the-ring trick," you tease. "Isn't that a little old-fashioned for a modern girl?"

"It's a lot quieter than an upper cut," Bronder explains.

Add 2 to your Karma points for defeating the HYDRA commander.

A rifle fires from above, and bullets ricochet off the shield you have hidden in your costume.

Turn to **69**.

209 Without meaning to, you fall asleep. By the time you wake up, night has fallen. Clipping your briefcase next to the phone-link computer interface built into the van, you pop open the briefcase's false bottom. Beneath it lies a portable terminal connecting you to the computer that records calls coming in to your nationwide hot line.

A network of volunteer computer operators called Stars and Stripes monitors all your calls and sorts the information for you. Only one new urgent call has come in since you checked this morning. At least, it seems urgent in its frequency.

Five times the computer printout of the message is the same: "I must speak with you personally, not with this machine. I'll call back in exactly one hour." *Curious,* you think.

The calls are recorded at fifteen, sixteen, seventeen, eighteen, and nineteen hundred hours. However, the last call was made at 19:45 and reads: "Forget it. The X-Men are taking care of it."

It is now past twenty hundred hours, and since the caller did not repeat his message on the last hour, you suppose your aid is no longer needed.

Curious, you wonder what it is the X-Men are taking care of, but since you have little contact with them, you realize you may never know. Your adventure has come to an end.

You may begin the adventure again, reducing your initial Karma and Health totals by one point each for your failure to recognize the importance of your physical well being.

You want to tell Bronder to leave you behind, **210** but you know she won't, so you must summon every ounce of strength to reach your companion.

Yanking on your shirt she hauls you into the chopper and buckles you in. As the helicopter rises and the cold, dark night air surrounds you, you pass into a different cold darkness.

When you awaken, you are lying in a hospital bed in SHIELD headquarters. Nick Fury and his agents, Hoffman and Bronder are seated by your side.

"How are you feeling, hero?" Laura Bronder asks with a smile.

"Sore," you answer truthfully. "What happened?"

"Laura's information led us to Viper's secret base in plenty of time. We recovered all of our rockets," Nick Fury fills you in, "but not, I'm afraid, the Viper."

"That teleporter makes her as slippery as her namesake," you note.

Fury nods. "But we also got the bonus of getting a HYDRA secret base, thanks to you and Laura."

"Always glad to be of service," you answer, smiling at Agent Bronder.

"The secret base was in Pittsburgh, under something called the Incline," Agent Bronder explains. "Some guy at the Incline told us you'd been there before."

"Yes," you reply, "with the Avengers."

"Well, we got you a little memento. Show him, Ken."

Agent Hoffman holds up a T-shirt with a picture of the Pittsburgh Incline. Underneath the picture, in ballpoint pen, are scrawled the words "I helped

SHIELD recover 574 rockets for the U.S. Government and all I got was this lousy T-shirt."

"Thank you," you laugh, and then wish you could stop because it hurts more than a little.

"The doctor said we shouldn't stay long," Fury says.

"You get better quick," Bronder orders.

"I think I will," you answer. The relief you feel knowing that Viper is no longer an immediate threat will go a long way toward helping you heal.

Your adventure is over. You may begin again, subtracting 2 points from your initial Health total but adding 1 point to your initial Karma total for your valiant efforts.

211 You slip up right next to Blacklash and level him with a karate chop. Lowering him gently to the ground, you check his eyes, breathing, and pulse to be sure he's out cold but not in any danger.

Turn to **28**.

212 Your charge has no more effect than to nudge the HYDRA commander back. But as his attention is turned to you, Agent Hoffman slams him over the head with his rifle butt, and the man slides to the floor. Add 1 to your Karma points for helping to defeat a high-level HYDRA operative. The other HYDRA agent in the room has been knocked unconscious—also by Hoffman.

Turn to **92**.

213 Launching a kick at Viper, you knock the deadly weapon from her hand, but she lashes out with a leg as well, connecting with your chest.

As you sprawl backward, she throws herself on top of you, her mouth opened wide. Not a moment too soon you remember the artificial fangs Viper wears in her mouth. You can see drops of lethal snake venom secretion glistening on the sharpened teeth.

She intends to poison me with a bite! you realize in disgust. In order to break away from Viper, you must make a Strength FEAT by rolling one die and adding the result to your Fighting ability. If the total is 8 or less, turn to **144**. If it is 9, turn to **27**. If it is 10 or more, turn to **126**.

Just as you are passing one of the entrances **214** to Central Park, you hear a beckoning whisper. "Pssst, Flagman . . . over here."

Warily eyeing the bushes where the voice came from, you step off the sidewalk onto the lush grass.

You make a sudden leap and catch hold of an overhanging tree branch, then pull yourself up. Perched high, you get a view of whoever or whatever is behind the bushes, without making yourself a target.

Beneath you, crouched low so as not to be seen, is a man in a highly unusual outfit—a blue body suit with orange sections, segmented to suggest a snake's ribs—an outfit you recognize.

"Schlichting! You? What do you want?" Suspicious, you wait for the man to reply. Frank Schlichting, alias the Constrictor, is a dangerous criminal and foe. Usually. There have been a few occasions when he has been helpful, though mostly for his own selfish reasons.

"Truce," Constrictor whispers hastily. "I've got some information for you."

"All right," you agree. You don't really trust this hood, but seeing that he is alone and obviously frightened and judging that you can easily outmaneuver him if he has foul play in mind, you see no harm in hearing him out.

"Would you come down from there? I don't want to call any attention to us."

You hesitate briefly, then jump down in front of your would-be informant.

Nervously Constrictor strokes the casings on his forearms. You know he can eject electrically charged whip-like cables from the casings if he plans to fight you. Instead, he whispers, "I wouldn't do this for anyone, but I owe ya one. Just don't think I'm turning into a fink or nothing."

"I wouldn't dream of it. What is it, Constrictor?"

"Only 'cause you saved my life, and 'cause she's crazy, you know?"

"Who's crazy?" you ask, growing impatient.

"A certain acquaintance of ours with green hair and lipstick."

"Viper? What's she up to?"

"I'm not sure exactly, but if you check out the Curtis Supply Warehouse in Newark at midnight you may see something that interests you, by the rocket's red glare."

"What's that supposed to mean? What will I see?"

"I don't know, exactly." The mercenary shrugs.

"Well, what makes you think I'll see anything at all?"

"I, uh, can't tell you that."

"Well, this is all very helpful, Constrictor," you reply, unable to keep the sarcasm out of your voice. "Why so nervous, Constrictor?"

"Are you kidding? If she finds out I've been talking to you, she's going to know something's up. I already helped you foil one of her plans, and you know what she's like."

You nod. The Viper is a vicious, ruthless international terrorist. She is undoubtedly one of your most terrifying foes. Her schemes almost always involve death and destruction on a massive scale, for the Viper is mad with the desire to annihilate everything you hold precious, and, most especially, she would like to crush the United States government.

"Why didn't you just leave a message on my hot line?" you ask. "Then you could have remained anonymous."

187

"Can't be too careful. Suppose she was listening in. She'd just change her plans. If she recognized my voice, she'd have me killed for sure. I'm hoping the witch'll just forget me, though I doubt I'll get that lucky."

"Don't you think you're being just a little bit paranoid, Constrictor?"

"No. She hates you for all the times you've defeated her. Tapping your hot line is just the kind of thing she might do to keep tabs on you."

You don't argue the point any further. After all, you remember, a mere high school student once broke into the hot line system, and though its security has been upgraded considerably, Viper is extremely formidable.

"How do I know that this isn't some sort of trick?" you ask.

"Look, I'm just tryin' to do you a favor. Take it or leave it," Constrictor hisses and starts to walk away.

"Schlichting?" you whisper after him. "Where can I reach you?"

"Are you kidding? As soon as I found out she was back in the country, I made arrangements with my travel agent. I'm blowing this coast until it cools off. If I could find a way off the planet, I might consider that, too. Good luck, Flagman. You'll need it."

You let Constrictor walk away without confronting him further. It's possible he's telling the truth, since he has helped you defeat Viper before. Yet, if Viper is truly involved, it would be just like her to use Constrictor to set you up. Constrictor could be in her pay, or an unwitting pawn.

At any rate, any scheme of the Viper's will be insidious, ending in global chaos if it isn't stopped. *The first question, though, you tell yourself, is will I be walking into a trap or really sneaking up on her plot?*

If you decide to follow Constrictor's tip and go to the Curtis Supply Warehouse in Newark, whether you think it's a trap or not, proceed to **192**. If you want to check out the warehouse but think you ought to get some help, turn to **129**.

Nick Fury comes pelting into the room, his **215** weapon drawn and ready. "I don't believe it!"

"Can I borrow your handcuffs?" you ask.

"Borrow away. Later, I'll have them bronzed for you," Fury replies. "After all these years, she's really been defeated."

"Have you recovered the rockets stored in the mines?" you ask, cuffing the villainess to the control panel.

"Yes. And Bronder and Hoffman managed to intercept some of the ones that were being beamed to Viper's new headquarters and sent them to our headquarters instead.

"You should be able to recover the rockets Viper sold, too. She had a list of sales in her computer, and I managed to prevent her from erasing the file."

"Jackpot!" Agent Hoffman cries when he comes up from behind Director Fury and sees your prisoner.

Bronder, just behind her partner, glances from Viper to you, a look of awe on her face.

"You don't look too happy," she notes.

"I'm relieved," you answer. "I just feel—we have scotched the snake, not killed it."

"Huh?"

"I think what Cap means," Fury explains, "is that madness like the Viper's remains in the world, whether we've captured her or not."

"Precisely," you reply. "There are hundreds of people in this country willing to buy rockets from Viper to use on someone else. They were ready to move down to her level of insanity to accomplish their goals, wrong or right. It's that kind of thinking that is far more dangerous than any single super-villain."

"You have a good point," Agent Hoffman says. "But I think we're all better off because you caught her."

"And there's always tomorrow to tackle the other problems," Agent Bronder adds.

"Both true," you add, feeling a little more light-hearted.

"And furthermore," Fury declares holding out his hand, "you'll always have us battling those problems alongside of you."

You accept the handshake with a grin. "What more could I ask for?"

Richard Carpenter's
ROBIN OF SHERWOOD

Gamebook 1:
THE KING'S DEMON
Graham Staplehurst

Have you ever wondered what it was like to be Robin
Hood, outlaw and protector of Sherwood Forest? Well,
here's your chance. In this gamebook YOU are Robin of
Sherwood, son of Herne the Hunter, champion of the poor
and oppressed. As you go through the book you make your
own choices and use your skill and judgement to outwit
your old enemy, the corrupt Sheriff of Nottingham and his
loathsome bullying servant, Sir Guy of Gisburne.

Gamebook 2:
THE SWORD OF THE TEMPLAR
Paul Mason

In this gamebook, the peace of the forest you love and the
lives of your companions are in danger. Your enemy is a
Knight Templar, Sir Roger of Ledbury, and the force he
wields threatens the very existence of Herne the Hunter!
Why does the Knight Templar so desire your downfall? Will
you be able to prevent him from achieving his goal, or has
Robin of Sherwood met his match? Even with your sword
Albion at your side, you will need all your strength and
resourcefulness to meet this challenge!